P9-CJV-453

SUPERSTATS
INCREDIBLE
BUGS

little bee books

A division of Bonnier Publishing
853 Broadway, New York, New York 10003

Project managed and commissioned by Dynamo Limited
Author: Moira Butterfield
Editor/Picture research: Dynamo Limited
Design: Dynamo Limited
Index: Marie Lorimer

Manufactured in China [025]

Printed in Guang Dong, China

First Edition: 10 9 8 7 6 5 4 3 2 1

Library of Congress Cataloging-in-Publication Data is available upon request.

ISBN 978-1-4998-0240-5

littlebeebooks.com

bonnierpublishing.com

SUPERSTATS INCREDIBLE BUGS

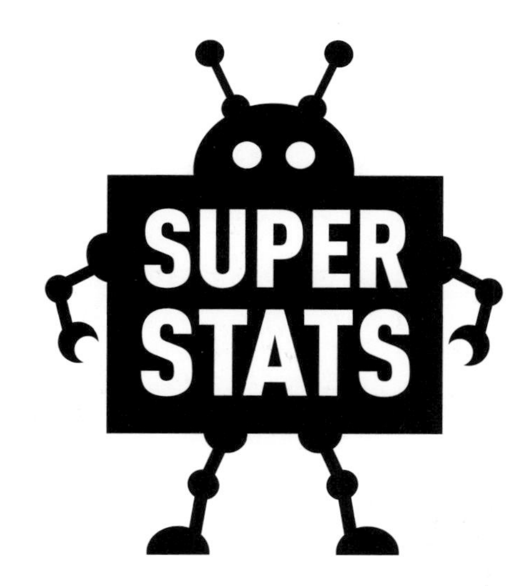

CONTENTS

AMAZING ANTS

Ants live everywhere on Earth except the very coldest, iciest spots. There are over 14,000 different species, from ants the size of a period to ants with heads as big as currants.

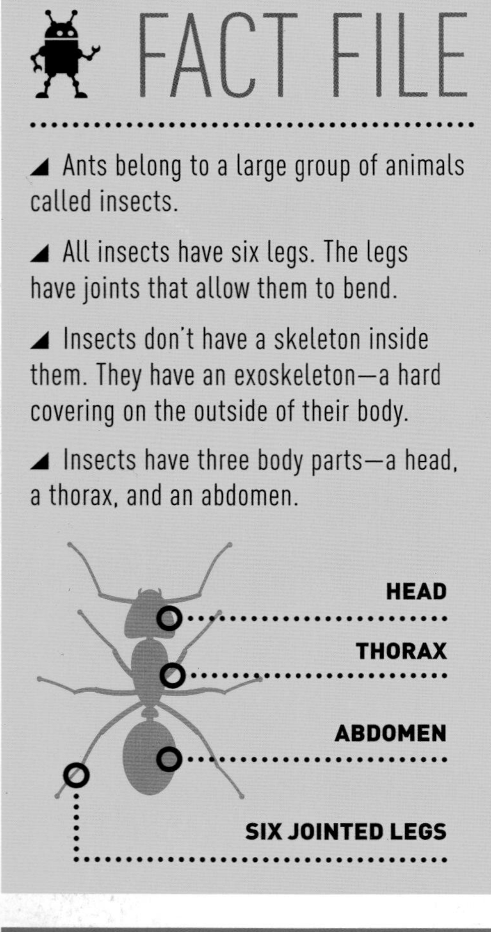

FACT FILE

- Ants belong to a large group of animals called insects.
- All insects have six legs. The legs have joints that allow them to bend.
- Insects don't have a skeleton inside them. They have an exoskeleton—a hard covering on the outside of their body.
- Insects have three body parts—a head, a thorax, and an abdomen.

OVER 100 MILLION YEARS AGO

Ants first appeared on Earth 100 million years ago in the time of the dinosaurs.

RED ANT

Some ants are armed with a sting, or they squirt out acid to defend themselves. Others bite!

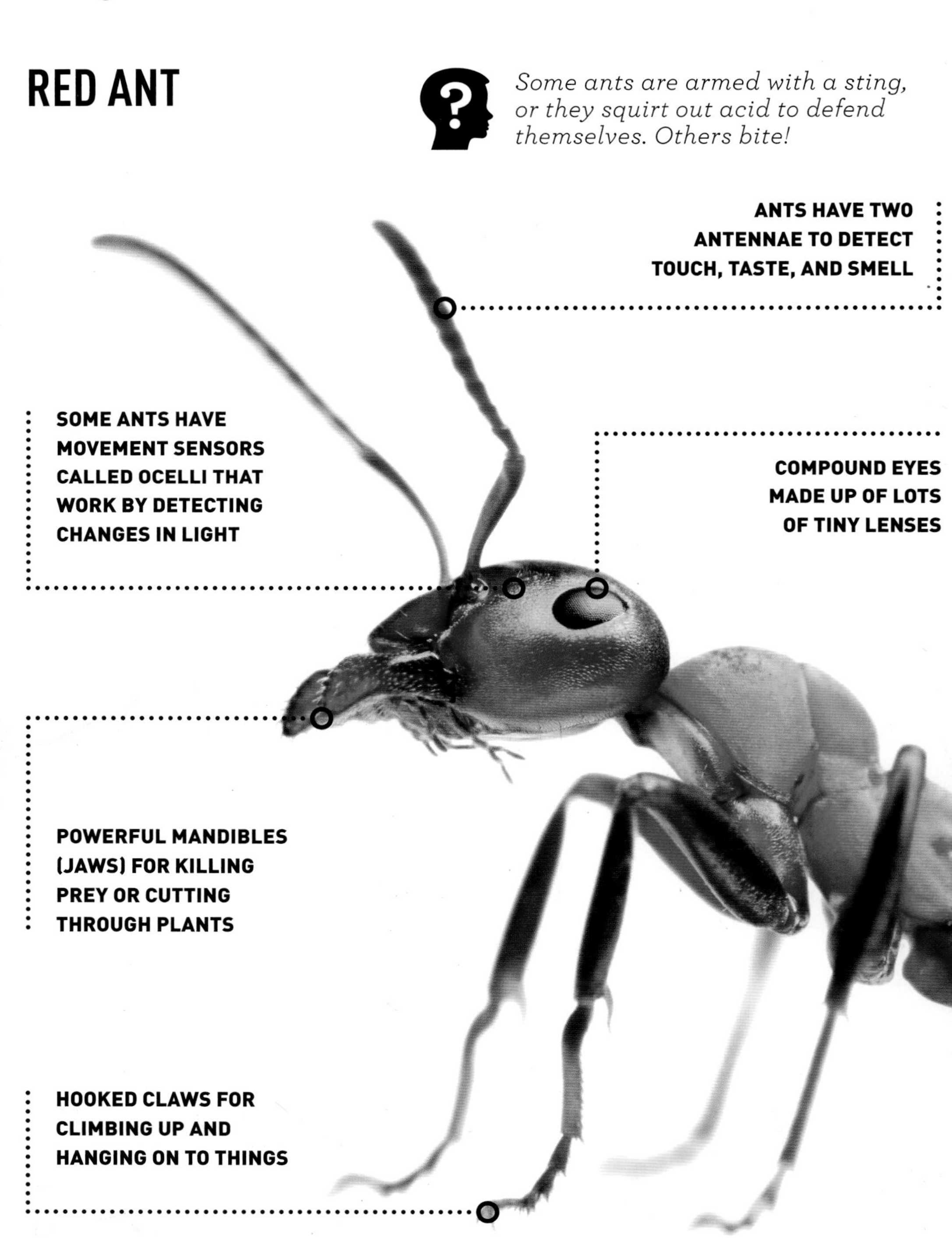

The sting of the South American **bullet ant** is said to be 30 times more painful than a bee sting.

BIGGEST *TO SMALLEST*

BULLET ANT *(WORKER)*
= 1.2 IN. LONG

CAREBARA ATOMA ANT *(WORKER)*
= 0.015 IN. LONG

ACTUAL SIZE

3,700 MILES

The length of the biggest mega-colony of ants ever found. It stretches from northern Italy along the Mediterranean coast to Spain. Amazingly, ants from one end of the colony can recognize ants from the other end.

1.5 *MILLION*

Scientists estimate there are at least 1.5 million ants on the planet for every human being.

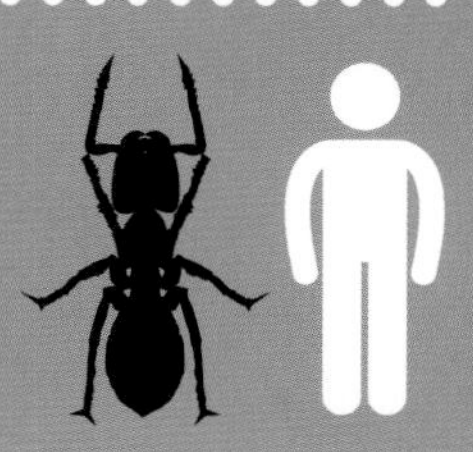

^ RED ANTS HERDING APHIDS

BUSY ANTS

SLAVERS

Some ants are slave-makers, stealing ants from other colonies and putting them to work.

HERDERS

Some ants keep herds of aphids, drinking the sugary nectar they make.

GROWERS

Some ants are farmers, growing edible fungus on rotting leaves in their nest.

THE HEART AND THE DIGESTIVE SYSTEM ARE IN THE ANT'S ABDOMEN

IT'S A RECORD!

2.4 INCHES LONG

The largest ant ever found—a fossil the size of a hummingbird. It roamed Wyoming nearly 50 million years ago.

STOMACH *x 2*

Worker ants have two stomachs. One contains food for themselves, and one stores food to give to larvae or queens in the colony.

THE LOVELY LADYBUG

Gardeners love ladybugs because they eat the little aphids that gobble up plants. You can even buy ladybugs and ladybug farm kits online. Just in case you decide to become a ladybug farmer, here are some facts about the unusual farm animals you'd be looking after.

7-SPOTTED LADYBUG

A ladybug is a type of insect called a beetle. A beetle has two sets of wings—forewings and hindwings. They vary from 0.08 inches to 0.4 inches long.

FACT FILE

The colors on ladybugs are designed to scare off enemies. They send a signal that the ladybug is poisonous.

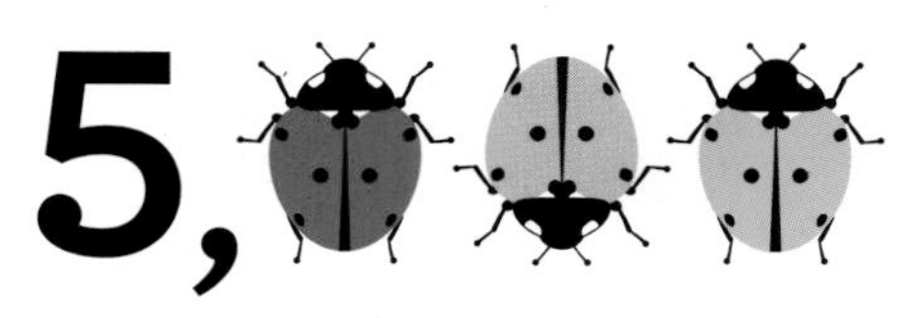

There are around 5,000 different types of ladybugs around the world. Some don't have spots.

Loveliness

A group of ladybugs is called a "loveliness" of ladybugs.

85 TIMES *PER SECOND*

The number of times a flying ladybug beats its wings.

IT'S A RECORD!

TOP ***SPOT!***

Subcoccinella 24-punctata *is the ladybug record-holder for the most spots. Unsurprisingly, it has 24 spots!*

5,000

The number of aphids that a hungry ladybug might consume in its lifetime.

Sometimes ladybugs play dead if they feel threatened.

LEAKING LEGS

If ladybugs are threatened, they can squeeze stinky yellow stuff out of their leg joints to repel predators.

NO *BIRTHDAYS*

Most ladybugs only live for one year.

THE FRIENDLY PEST

Cockroaches are gross, right? Unfair! Not all cockroaches are bad. In fact, they're kind to each other and live together in peace and harmony. Just don't tread on one in the night. They're pretty crunchy...

FACT FILE

- Cockroaches are nocturnal. They come out at night to find food and water. In the daytime, they hide in crevices.
- Cockroaches eat anything starchy. They have tiny bacteria living inside their cells that provide them with all the vitamins they need. So they don't have to bother eating a balanced, healthy diet like we do.

COMMON AMERICAN COCKROACH

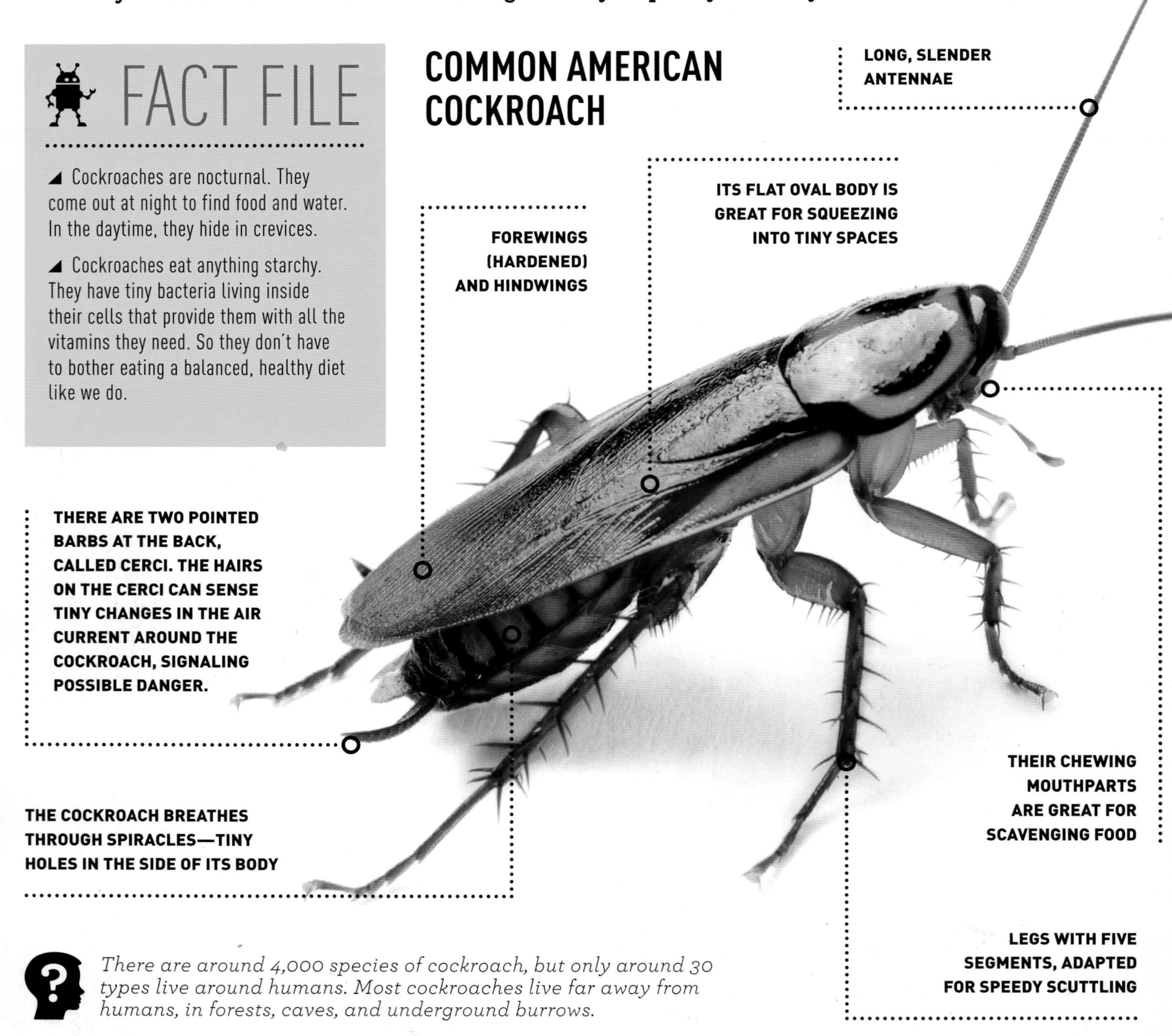

There are around 4,000 species of cockroach, but only around 30 types live around humans. Most cockroaches live far away from humans, in forests, caves, and underground burrows.

^ MADAGASCAR HISSING COCKROACH

WHAT'S THAT NOISE?

The **Madagascar hissing cockroach** makes a good pet. It fires air out of tiny holes along its body to make a noise.

Cockroaches are farmed in China to use in medicines and as crunchy fried snacks.

3.4 MILES *PER HOUR*

Top speed of a the **American cockroach,** one of the fastest insects in the world.

IT'S A RECORD!

HEAVIEST

The rhino cockroach grows up to 1.3 oz. It lives in Queensland, Australia, and it's the biggest cockroach in the world.

TINY HI-TECH

Scientists can remote-control cockroaches to send them into hard-to-reach places. They strap a tiny camera to the cockroach's back and stimulate it to turn left, right, or stop.

50

Up to 50 babies may hatch from one cockroach egg capsule, called an ootheca.

6 WEEKS

The amount of time some species can survive without food. A cockroach can live for at least a week with no head.

FOLLOW THE TRAIL

If a cockroach finds food, it may lay a trail of smelly poop for its friends to follow, leading them to the treat.

Cockroaches live in family groups and can recognize their relatives. They have been found to have personality traits, too. Some are shy and cautious. Others are confident explorers.

BUSY BEES

On a sunny summer's day you might see honey bees out and about, collecting sugary nectar and yellow pollen from flowers. They will take it back to their hive to eat straight away or to make into honey for food during the winter months.

INSIDE A BEEHIVE

FACT FILE

1. To make honey, a bee sucks nectar from flowers. She carries the nectar home in a special honey stomach.

2. She passes the nectar on to other bees, who chew it for a while to help turn it into honey before they pour it into the honeycomb, where it gradually dries and becomes thick.

3. The bees help it to dry by fanning it with their wings.

4. When the honey is ready, the bees seal the honeycomb with wax, storing the honey for use later.

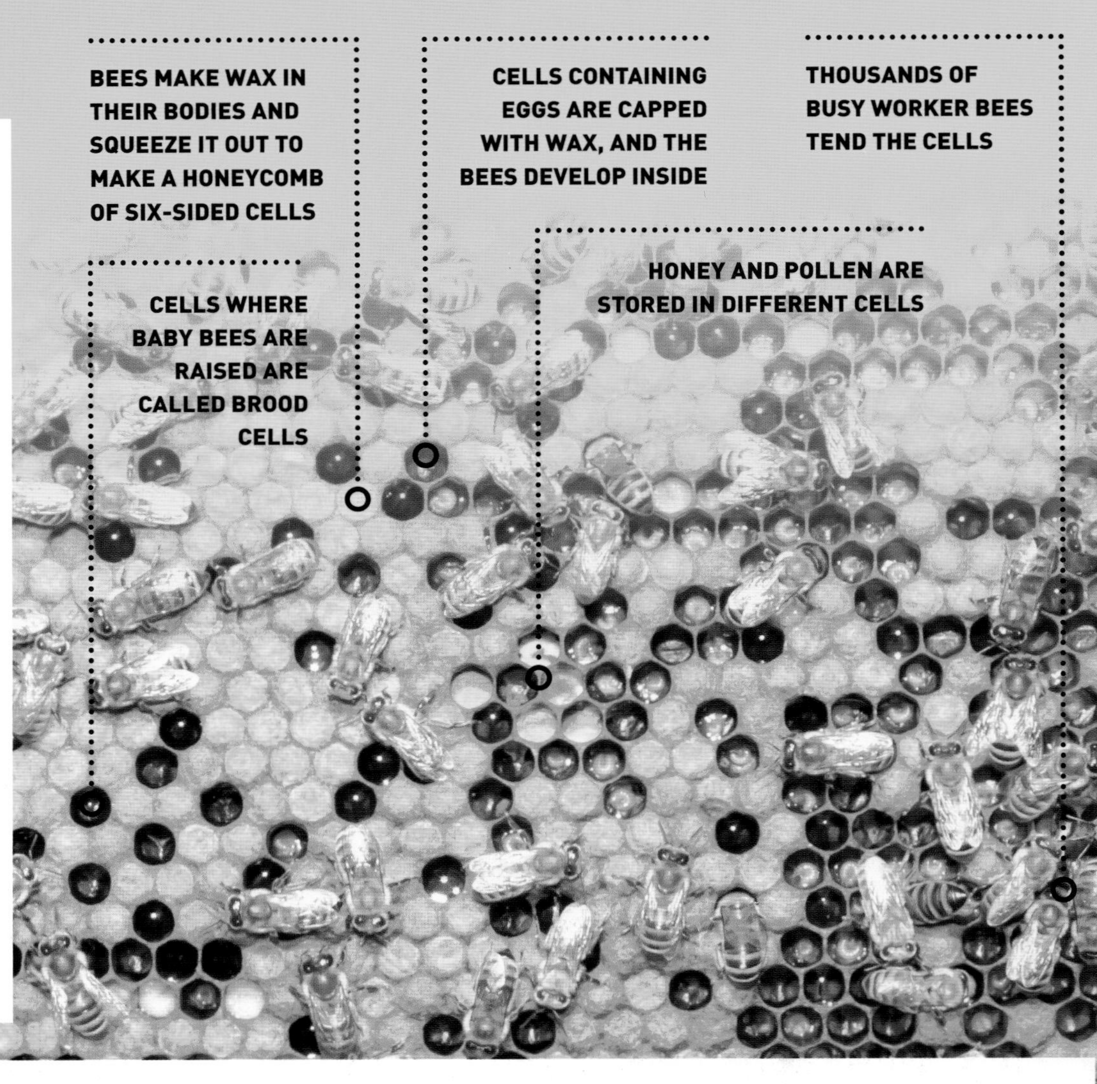

WHO'S WHO?

QUEEN

Bigger than all the other bees in the hive, this feisty female lives for up to three years.

WORKER

Females who collect nectar and pollen, feed the babies, build the honeycomb, and make honey. They live for about five weeks.

DRONES

Males whose only job is to mate with the queen. They can't sting. They get thrown out at the end of summer to die.

50 *to* 100

The number of flowers a bee will visit on one flight.

2,000

The number of eggs a queen can lay in a day.

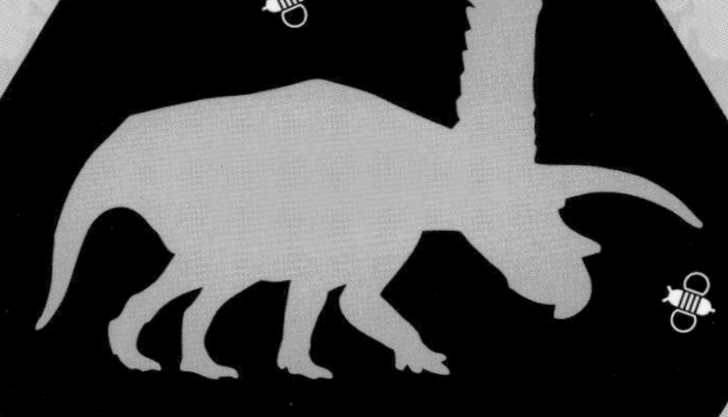

Bees lived in the time of the dinosaurs.

Bees are fantastic at smelling and have even been trained to sniff out explosives!

20,000 *to* 60,000

The number of bees in one colony.

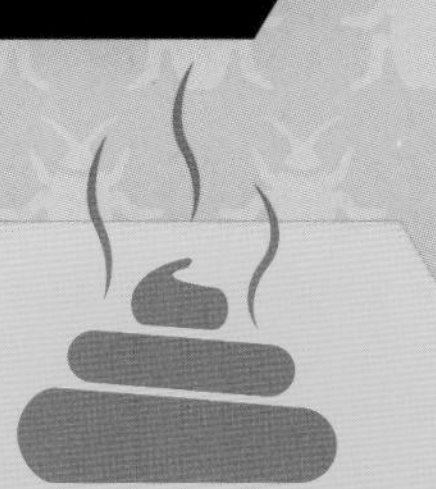

Bees poop outside their hive or in a corner far away from the honeycombs.

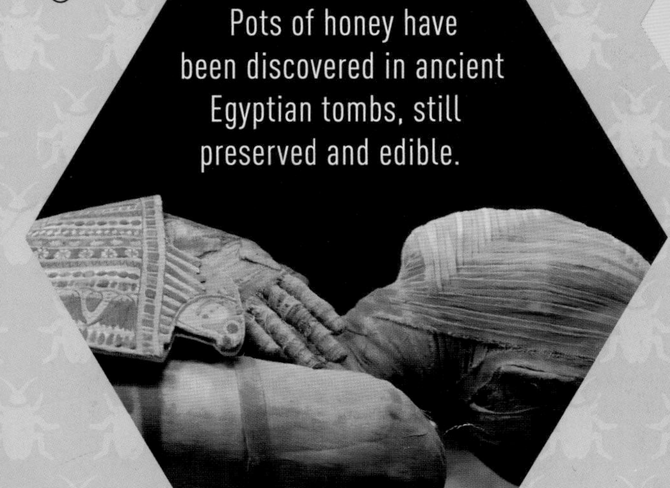

Pots of honey have been discovered in ancient Egyptian tombs, still preserved and edible.

200 BEATS PER SECOND

The number of times a flying bee beats its wings every second (which makes its buzzing noise).

ITCHING AHEAD

Be warned, these pages will make you scratch! They're all about head lice—tiny wingless insects that live on the human head. Why? Because it's just the place to give them a ready supply of their favorite food—human blood.

FACT FILE

LOUSE EGGS

1. Female lice lay eggs on hair, near the scalp.

2. They secrete a glue to stick an egg to a hair strand.

3. After 6–10 days, a new louse hatches.

4. The empty egg goes white. It is called a nit.

HEAD LOUSE

Itching is an allergic reaction to the saliva (spit) the louse dribbles into its bite to keep blood flowing.

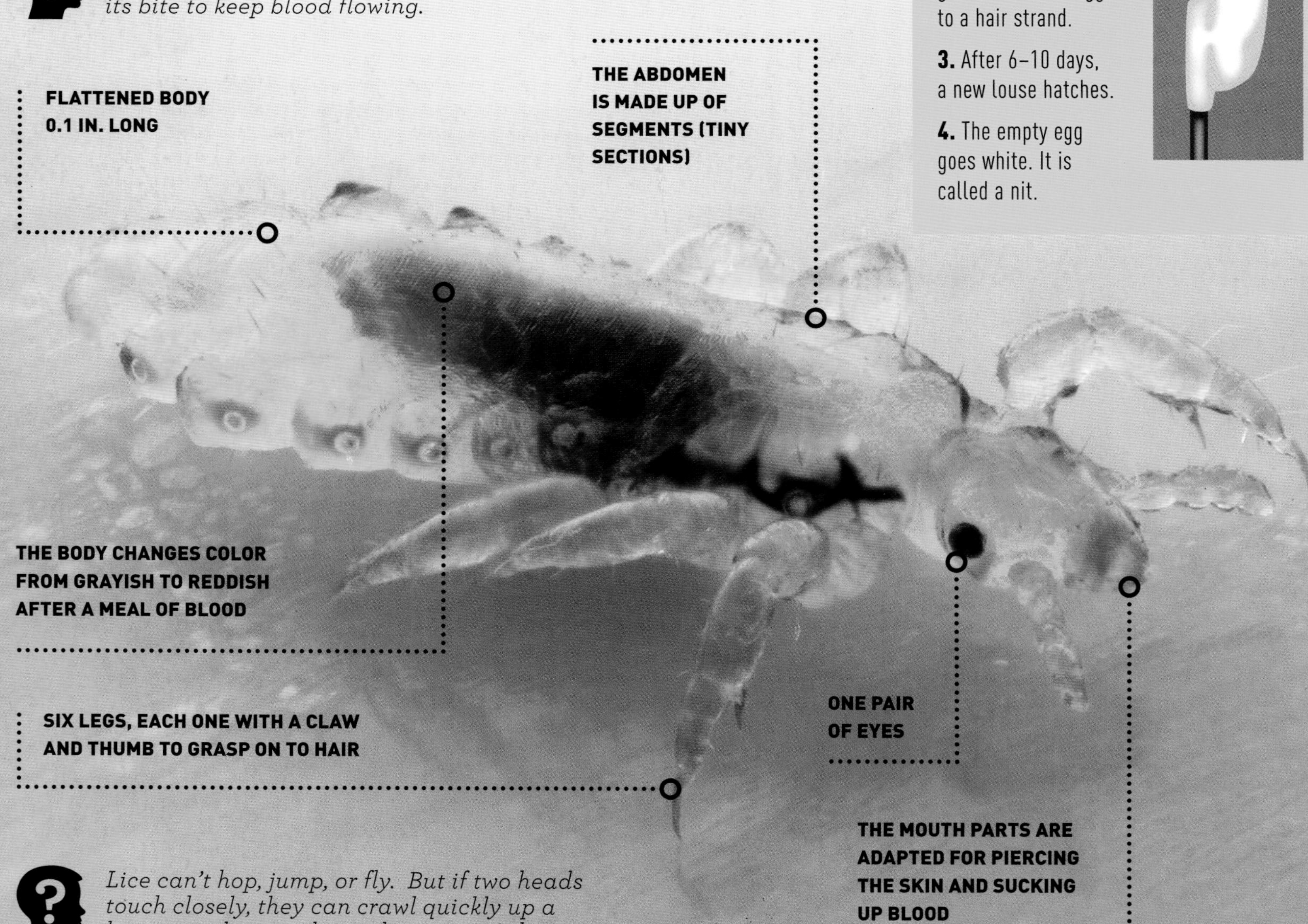

Lice can't hop, jump, or fly. But if two heads touch closely, they can crawl quickly up a hair strand to reach another person's hair.

10–12 *MILLION*

The number of people infected with head lice each year in the USA.

TEENSY *BUT ITCHY*

An egg is about the same size as the tip of a pencil.

A louse is around the size of a sesame seed.

4–5 *TIMES A DAY*

How many times a head louse bites the skin to feed on blood.

A female head louse lays 3–4 eggs a day.

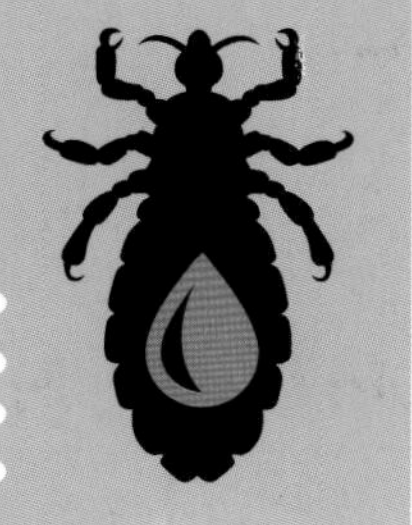

48 HOURS

The amount of time a louse can live off a head, for example on a hairbrush or pillow.

30 DAYS

How long a head louse lives.

Head lice are sometimes found on ancient Egyptian mummies, along with ancient nit combs buried in their tombs.

AGES 4–14

The age bracket most likely to get head lice.

Girls are 2–4 times more likely to get head lice than boys because they have longer hair.

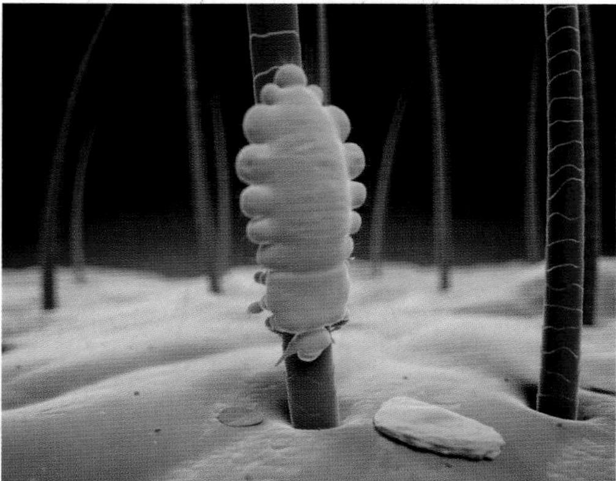

Head lice (left) are harmless. They don't pass on diseases. They may even help people become immune to more harmful lice.

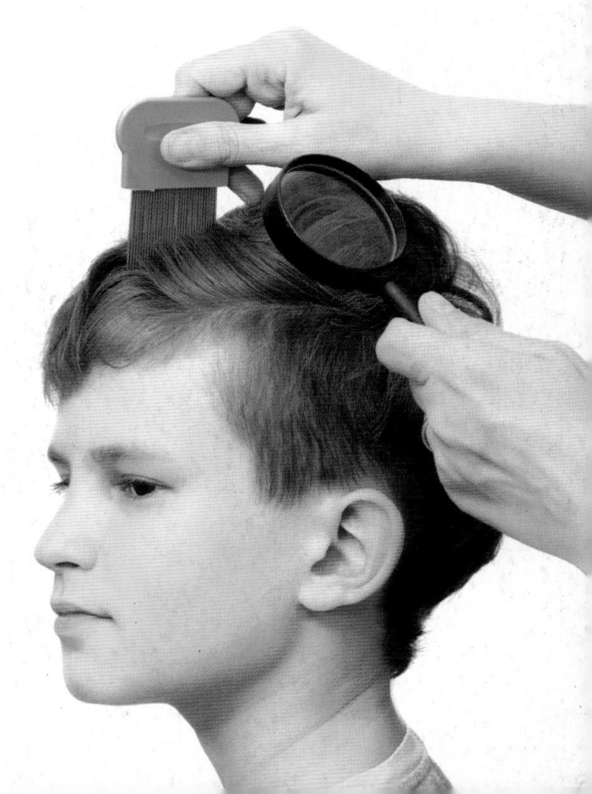

LICE DNA

Archaeologists love head lice—or at least their ancient remains. By testing the head lice DNA they can match related head lice in different locations to learn more about the journeys groups of ancient humans took.

WILY WASPS

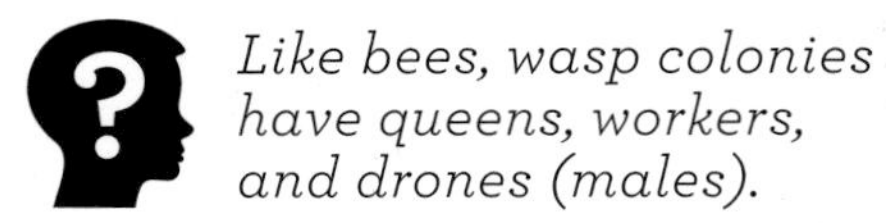

Like bees, wasp colonies have queens, workers, and drones (males).

There are around 30,000 different kinds of wasps. Some are harmless non-stingers, while others have painful stings. Be sure to know which is which!

YELLOW JACKET WASP

WASPS HAVE A WAIST CALLED A PETIOLE

WASPS HAVE COMPOUND EYES MADE UP OF MANY LENSES (SEE PG. 36), PLUS SOME TINY MOVEMENT SENSORS CALLED OCELLI

TWO PAIRS OF WINGS

WASPS HAVE BRIGHT STRIPES TO WARN PREDATORS THAT THEY TASTE BAD. WASPS WITH STINGERS HAVE THE BRIGHTEST COLORS.

POINTED LOWER ABDOMEN

THE MOUTHPARTS ARE ADAPTED FOR CHEWING AND LICKING. WASPS CAN'T SWALLOW THEIR FOOD. THEY CHEW IT UP AND FEED IT TO THEIR LARVAE. IN RETURN, THEY DRINK THE SUGARY LIQUID THE LARVAE MAKE.

ONLY FEMALE WORKER WASPS HAVE STINGERS, AT THE BACK OF THEIR BODY

Some wasps don't build nests. They live in holes and crevices. They attack their prey, paralyze it with a sting, and lay their eggs on it. When they hatch, the larvae will eat the paralyzed prey alive.

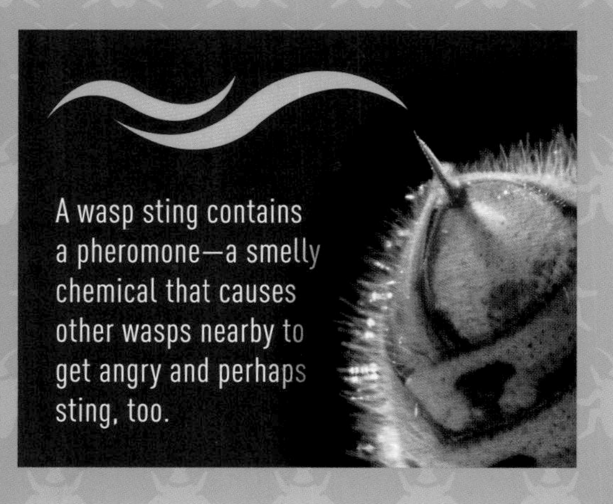

A wasp sting contains a pheromone—a smelly chemical that causes other wasps nearby to get angry and perhaps sting, too.

COLOR = PAIN

Wasps aren't all black and yellow. Some are bright red or metallic blue. The most colorful ones generally have stingers.

^ TARANTULA HAWK WASP

5,000

The estimated population of a wasp colony at its peak in late summer.

^ ASIAN GIANT HORNET

THE BIG ONES

TARANTULA HAWK WASP

This wasp (above) is from New Mexico. It lays its eggs on tarantula spiders, paralyzed by its sting.

ASIAN GIANT HORNET

These (left) are found in northwest China and can kill people with their sting.

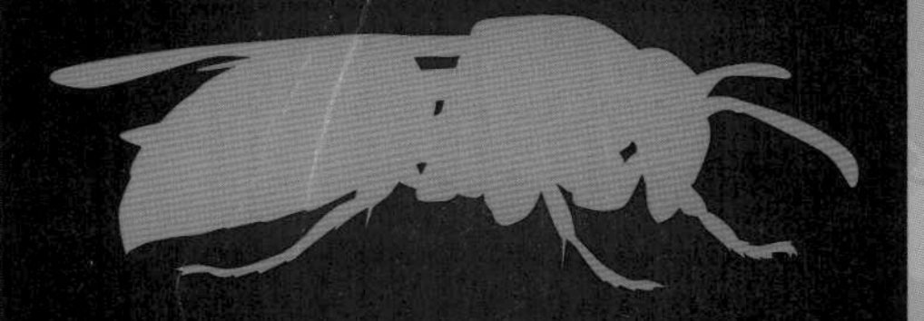

ACTUAL SIZE

= BOTH UP TO **2 IN. LONG**

BYE, GUYS

Only queen wasps survive winter. Workers and drones die. Some wasps live in nests (below) with six-sided cells for their larvae. They build it from wood pulp, gathered by the wasps and chewed to make it soft. They carry home meat for the larvae to eat.

IT'S A RECORD!

220 lb.

Weight of the world's biggest empty wasp nest, found in Tasmania. It would have been home to around 100,000 wasps. It was found by a 12-year-old boy.

ME TOO!

In Native American legend, the bees of the world asked Wakonda, the Great Spirit, to give them a stinger. The bees told everyone that they were going to get stingers, and the wasps heard about it—so they turned up on the same day as the bees and got stingers, too.

THE MINI ONES

The world's smallest insects are tiny **FAIRYFLY WASPS.** The tiniest of all is just 130 microns long. A human hair is about 100 microns wide.

ACTUAL SIZE

CAN YOU SEE THIS DOT?
IT IS THE SIZE OF FAIRYFLY WASP!

= 130 MICRONS LONG

CRAZY CATERPILLARS

Caterpillars are the larvae (babies) of butterflies. They come in all kinds of incredible shapes and sizes!

LIFE CYCLE OF A BUTTERFLY

1. A butterfly lays its eggs in a safe place under a leaf. The eggs hatch into caterpillars.

2. A caterpillar eats as much as it can, molting (losing its skin and regrowing a new one) several times as it grows.

3. It stops eating and either spins itself a shiny cocoon or creates a hard chrysalis shell around itself to prepare for metamorphosis (a process to change its body shape completely)

4. The caterpillar digests itself, releasing chemicals that dissolve it into caterpillar soup. Only a few groups of important cells, called imaginal discs, remain.

5. The imaginal discs grow into new butterfly body parts, using the dissolved cell soup as food energy.

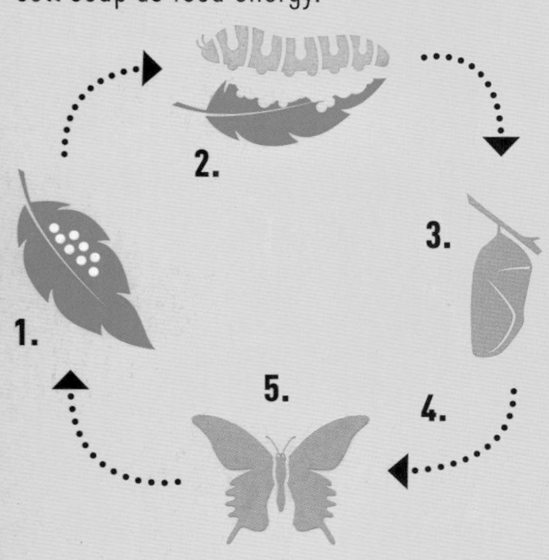

SADDLEBACK CATERPILLAR

CATERPILLAR SPECIES ALL LOOK VERY DIFFERENT. THE SADDLEBACK CATERPILLAR GROWS TO ABOUT 0.8 IN. LONG

THE SADDLEBACK CATERPILLAR HAS FLESHY HORNS CALLED TUBERCLES, WHICH ARE ARMED WITH SPINES TO PACK A PAINFUL STING, BUT NOT ALL CATERPILLARS STING

MOST CATERPILLARS EAT ONLY PLANTS AND HAVE MOUTH PARTS FOR MUNCHING PLANT MATERIAL

TUBE-SHAPED SEGMENTED BODY (MADE UP OF SECTIONS)

THE SADDLEBACK HAS SUCKERS ON ITS PROLEGS, BUT SOME CATERPILLARS HAVE HOOKLETS, LIKE THE HOOKS ON VELCRO

IT'S A RECORD!

4.5 *INCHES*

The size of a giant atlas moth caterpillar (right). It is the largest caterpillar in the world. It can spray stinking fluid up to 20 in. away to defend itself.

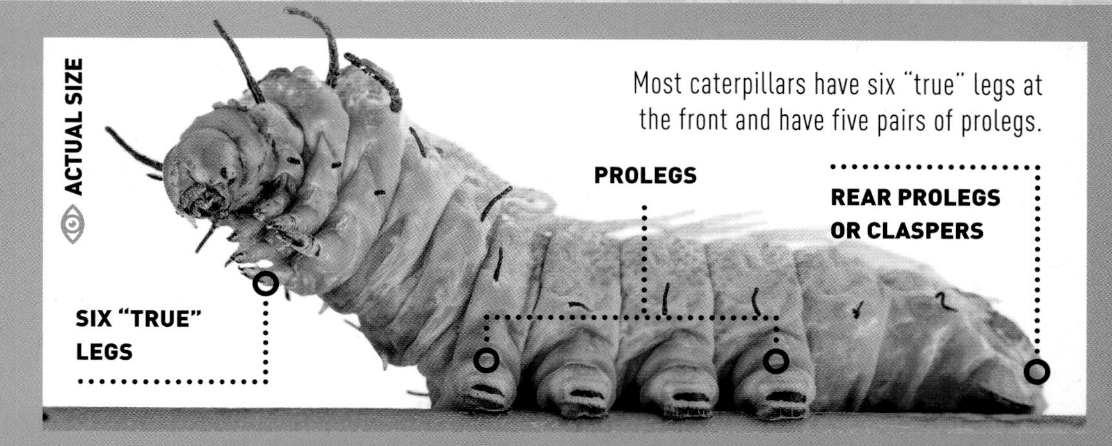

180,000+

Types of caterpillar so far discovered. Hawaii is the only place known to have meat-eating hunter caterpillars.

Some caterpillars are camouflaged to look just like twigs.

FAMILY MEAL

Sometimes caterpillars, such as **monarchs**, are cannibals. They will eat the eggs of their own kind.

Some caterpillars are marked with big spots that look like eyes. This makes them look like a bigger creature to possible attackers.

POISON!

Five- and six-spot burnet caterpillars contain cyanide poison from the plants they eat. That puts off would-be predators!

BEAUTIFUL BUTTERFLIES

Butterflies feed on the nectar that flowers make, so you are most likely to see them when the weather is warm and flowers are blooming.

BLUE MORPHO

Blue morpho butterflies (right) are among the largest butterflies in the world, with a wingspan (the measurement from wingtip to wingtip) of up to 8 in. They live in the tropical forests of Latin America.

- Butterfly wings are coated with many thousands of tiny transparent scales.
- The scales aren't brightly colored. They only appear to be bright and shiny because of the way that light bounces back off from them.
- A butterfly's color attracts mates. Bright colors can also send a signal to enemies—*"I'm poisonous. Don't eat me!"*

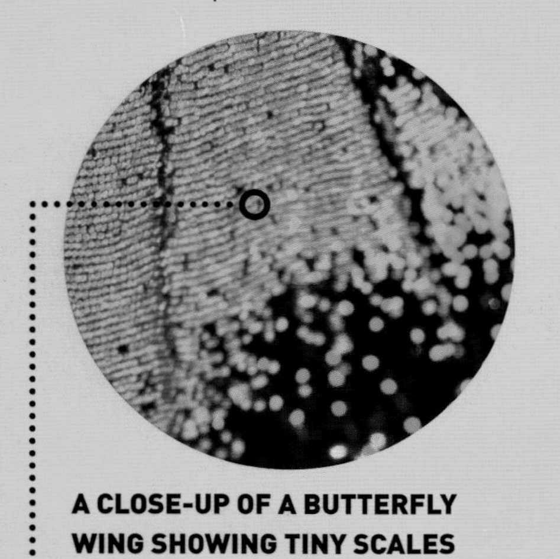

A CLOSE-UP OF A BUTTERFLY WING SHOWING TINY SCALES

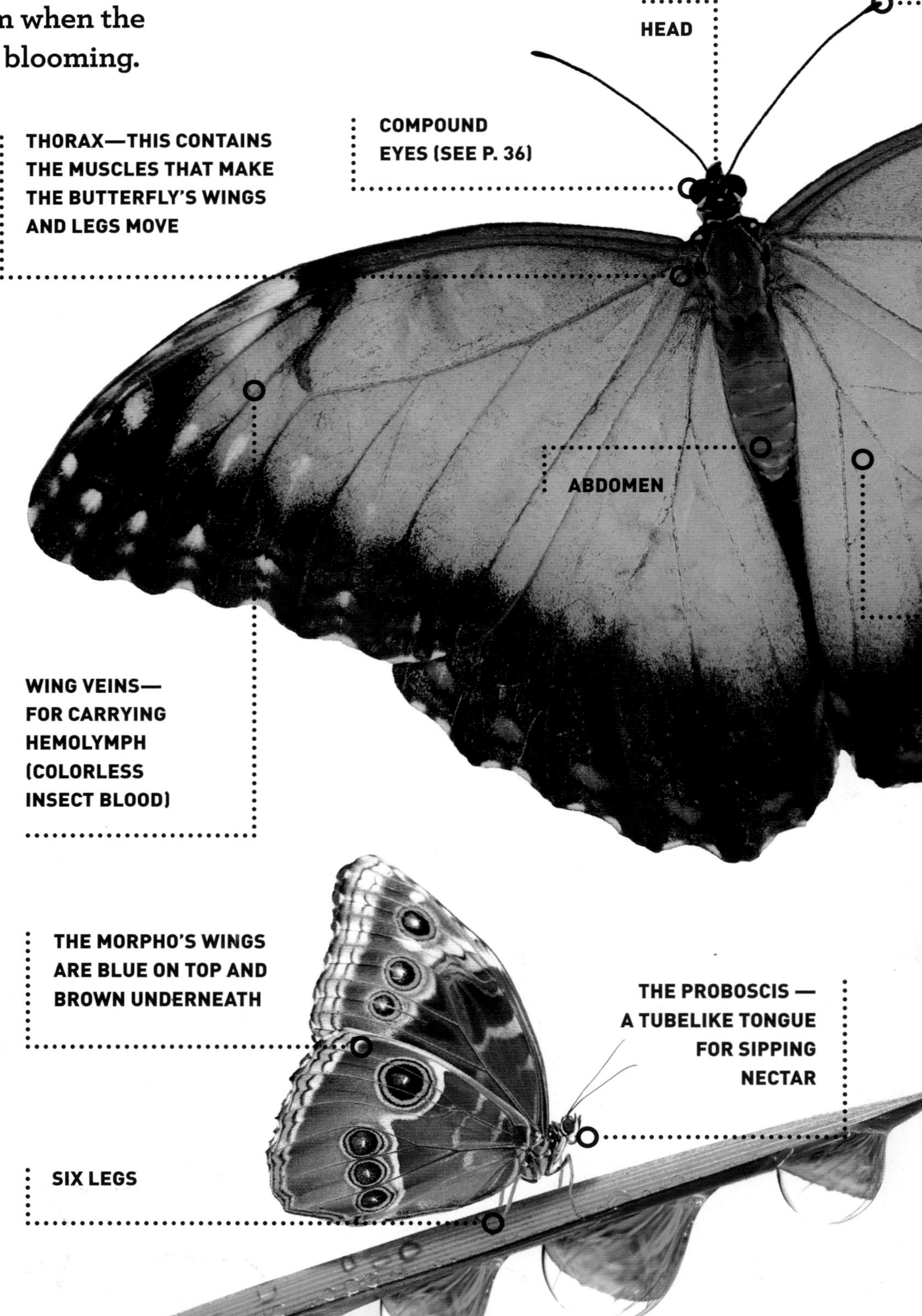

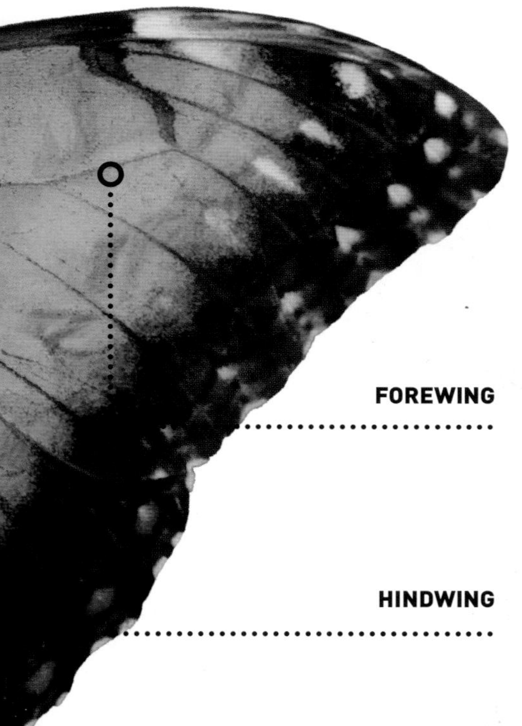

17,500

The approximate number of butterfly species we know about. There are probably many still to be discovered.

FINDING FLOWERS

Many flowers have "nectar guides"—line patterns on them that guide a butterfly toward the nectar in the middle.

Butterflies seem to particularly like pink, red, yellow, and white flowers.

IS IT A ***LEAF?***

Leaf butterflies have a great disguise to hide from their enemies. Their wings are colored and shaped to make them look just like dead leaves.

12.5 in.

The wingspan of the female **Queen Alexandra's birdwing**, the world's largest butterfly. That's bigger than most rulers! It lives in tropical New Guinea.

0.62 in.

The wingspan of the world's smallest butterfly, the **western pygmy blue,** found in the western USA. That's about the size of an adult human's thumbnail.

30 MPH

The flight speed of the fastest butterflies. Species of butterflies called **skippers** are the speediest.

2,000 *MILES +*

The distance some **monarch** butterflies migrate (journey) every fall, from Canada to Mexico.

6–12 *MONTHS*

The lifespan of the longest-living butterflies (such as **monarchs**). Some butterflies only live as adults for a few days.

HAIRY FLIERS

Moths are the hairy, fat relatives of the butterflies. There are around 160,000 different species—many more than butterflies. They live all over the world.

CECROPIA MOTH

THE MOTH IN THIS PICTURE IS A CECROPIA MOTH. IT LIVES IN NORTH AMERICA AND MEASURES UP TO 7 IN. ACROSS

A MOTH'S ANTENNAE ARE FEATHERY AND COMBLIKE, UNLIKE THE CLUB-SHAPED TIPS OF BUTTERFLY ANTENNAE

MOTHS HAVE NO NOSES. THEY SMELL BY SENSING SCENT MOLECULES IN THE AIR USING THEIR ANTENNAE.

LIKE BUTTERFLIES, SOME MOTHS HAVE FALSE EYE PATTERNS TO MAKE THEM LOOK BIGGER AND SCARE OFF ENEMIES

FOREWINGS AND HINDWINGS HAVE A SECTION THAT CONNECTS THEM CALLED A FRENULUM. BUTTERFLIES DON'T HAVE FRENULUMS

MOTHS HAVE THOUSANDS OF TINY WING SCALES, SIMILAR TO A BUTTERFLY

A MOTH'S BODY IS STOUTER AND HAIRIER THAN A BUTTERFLY'S, AND THE HAIRS HELP KEEP THE MOTH WARM AT NIGHT

Not all moths are nocturnal (night flying). In fact, there are more moths flying during the day than butterflies.

When they rest, moths spread their wings flat or flatten them against their body. Butterflies fold their wings upward.

BIGGEST *TO SMALLEST*

ATLAS MOTH
= 1 FT. *WINGSPAN*

(Above) The female Atlas moth, the biggest moth of all, is found in southeast Asia.

NEPTICULID MOTH
= 0.1 IN. *WINGSPAN*

Nepticulid moths are the smallest moths of all. They live between leaf layers, munching outward on the leaf.

^ TULIP-TREE BEAUTY MOTH

IT'S A RECORD! *FASTEST* FLYING INSECT

At 33 mph, the sphinx moth is one of the fastest of all flying insects.

Luna moths have no mouth, so they can't eat. They live for one week—just long enough to mate and die.

Moths pollinate the flowers they visit to sip nectar. Most nighttime moths visit fragrant white flowers (below). They are easier to see and smell in the dark.

HIDE *AND SEEK*

Some moths mimic other things to scare off predators, or are camouflaged to look like bark or leaves.

WOOD NYMPH MOTHS
These look like dollops of bird poop!

TARANTULA MOTHS
These mimics look like big spiders.

CLEARWING MOTHS (below)
These look like wasps.

Moths outnumber butterflies by around 10 to 1.

^ PRIVET-HAWKMOTH

DRACULA'S MOTH

The **death's-head hawkmoth** has a skull pattern on its body. That's why it often appears in horror stories, such as *Dracula* by Bram Stoker.

7 MILES

How far away a male moth can smell a female moth.

Why do moths fly toward artificial light? Nobody knows for sure!

I'M JUST A STICK!

Stick insects and leaf insects belong to a group of insects called phasmids, which has around 2,500 species. They are the master disguise artists of the insect world. Their name—phasmid—means ghostlike, because they are as tough to see as a ghost!

SOME ADULT STICK INSECTS HAVE WINGS

NORTHERN WALKING STICK INSECT

Can you figure out which end is the head and which end is the tail? It's tricky!

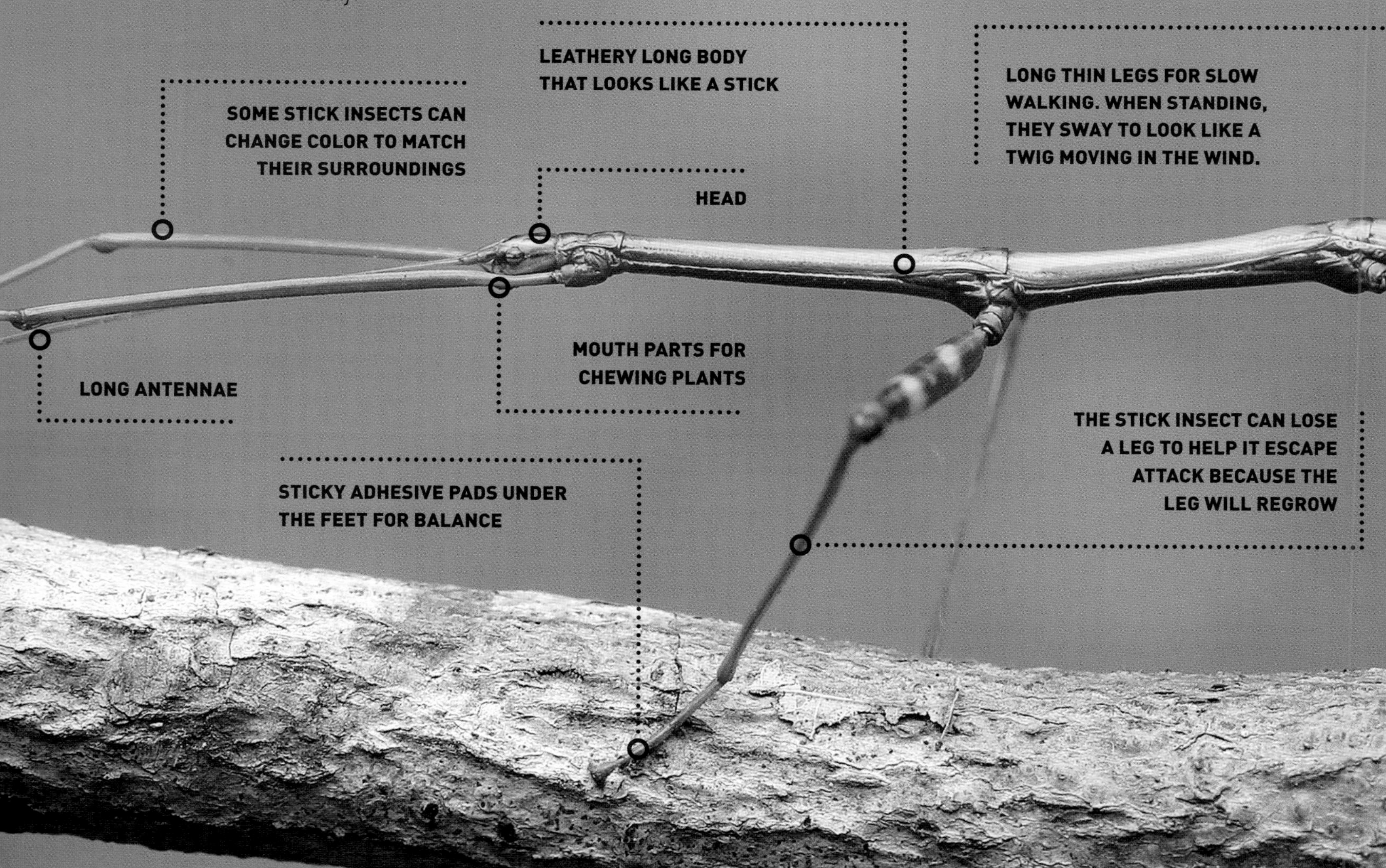

Stick insect eggs look like seeds so that hungry predators won't notice them on the forest floor.

GIRLS RULE

Female stick insects can reproduce without males. Some species have no known male.

IT'S A RECORD!

22-*INCH* MEGASTICK

The world's longest insect is the Chan's megastick, found in Borneo. With its legs extended, the female is 22 in. long.

50+

The number of **leaf insect** species in the world. They have body parts that look like leaves, including leaflike veins.

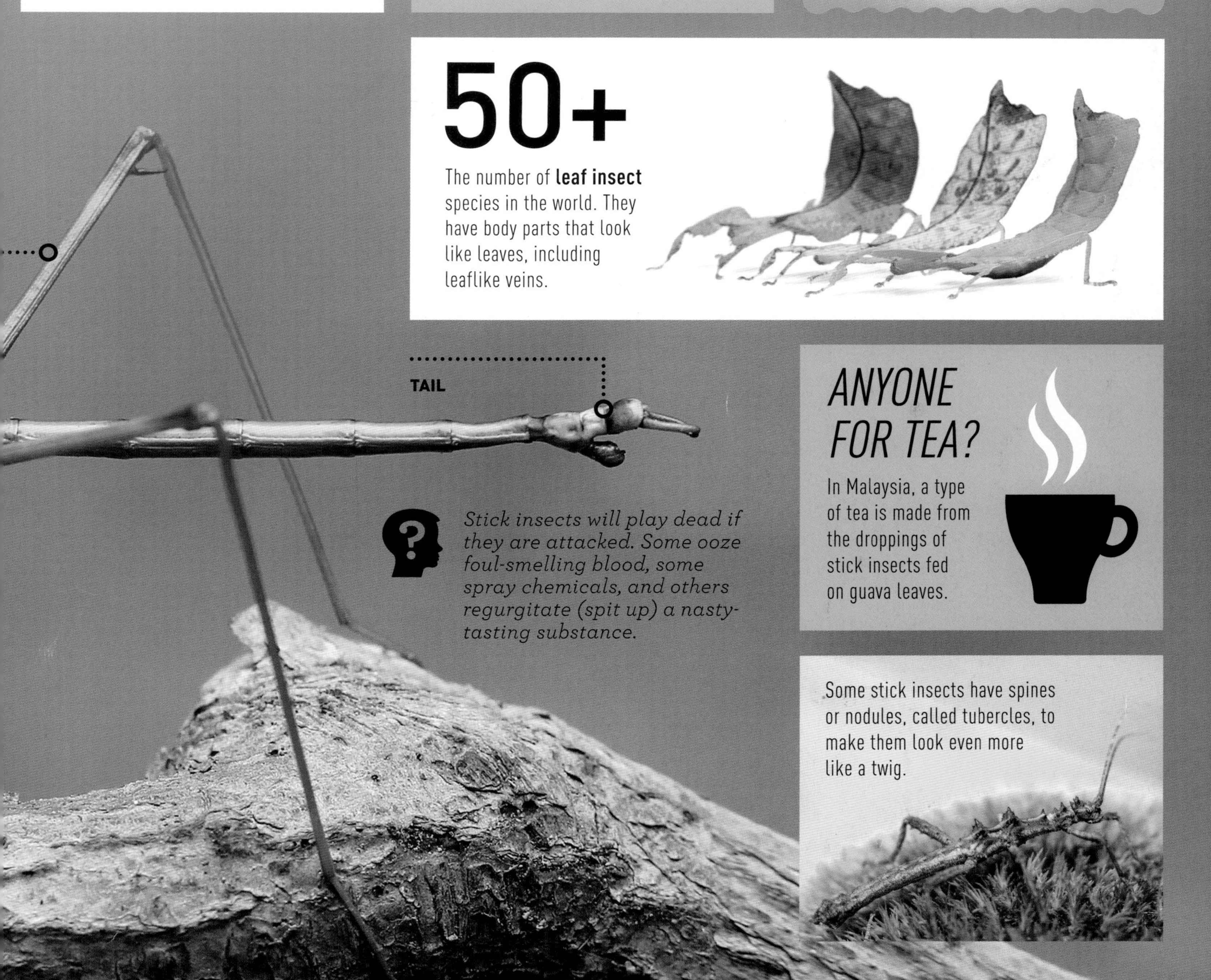

Stick insects will play dead if they are attacked. Some ooze foul-smelling blood, some spray chemicals, and others regurgitate (spit up) a nasty-tasting substance.

ANYONE FOR TEA?

In Malaysia, a type of tea is made from the droppings of stick insects fed on guava leaves.

Some stick insects have spines or nodules, called tubercles, to make them look even more like a twig.

FIGHT!

Rhino beetles are found everywhere except Antarctica. The males are the super-strong wrestlers of the insect world.

HERCULES BEETLE

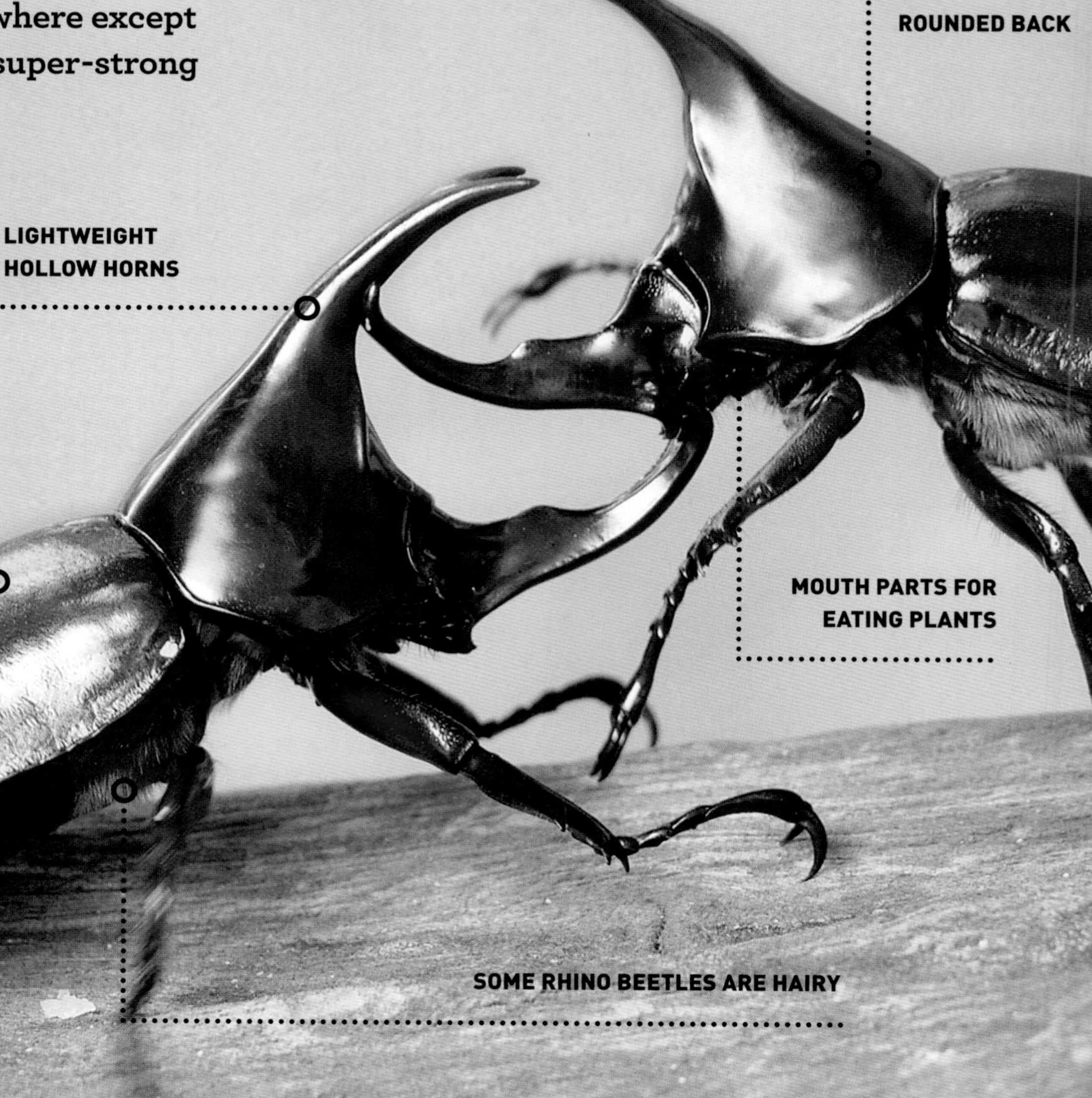

FACT FILE

FIGHTING FACTS

Different types of male rhino beetle have different fighting styles, depending on their horn shape.

1. Hercules beetles get their opponent in a full body hold to push them away.

2. Japanese rhino beetles slide their upward-curving horn under their opponent to flip it.

Rhino beetles come in different colors. They can be brown, black, gray, or green. Some look metallic.

The males don't kill each other in their fights. They just push each other away from the females they want to mate with.

3. Caliper beetles fence each other with their narrow serrated horns.

PET *BEETLES*

Rhino beetles are popular pets in Japan. They are even sold in vending machines.

300+

Number of known rhino beetle species.

MUSHI KING IS A POPULAR BEETLE COLLECTING AND SWAPPING CARD GAME IN JAPAN.

THE BIGGEST, STRONGEST RHINO BEETLES CAN FETCH THOUSANDS OF DOLLARS IN JAPAN. THEY ARE NICKNAMED "BLACK DIAMONDS."

^ JAPANESE RHINOCEROS BEETLE

BIG *BABIES*

Some rhino beetles live as larvae for up to seven years before they become adult beetles. These big beetle larvae (below) look like giant, freaky caterpillars the size of a child's hand.

ACTUAL SIZE

SCHOOL DUEL

In Japan's National Rhino Beetle Sumo Championship, schools bring their beetles to compete. The beetles must push each other off a pole.

850x

The **Hercules beetle** can lift 850 times its own weight. That's the equivalent of a human lifting nine adult African elephants!

ROLL WITH IT

Meet the world's strongest insect, the best insect mother, and some incredible mini navigators—all of them poop-eaters! Welcome to the wonderful world of the dung beetles.

DUNG BEETLE

Dung beetles are in a family of beetles called scarabs. So are the rhino beetles (see pg. 26). There are lots of different species of dung beetle. They live everywhere except the frozen wastes of Antarctica (there's not enough animal poop there).

2 HOURS

The approximate length of time it takes dung beetles to remove a 3 lb. pile of elephant dung. Around 16,000 beetles would do it.

DUNG BEETLES CAN GROW UP TO 2.3 IN. LONG

THEY HAVE LONG WINGS FOLDED UNDER HARD WING-CASES

A ROUGH BODY SURFACE PREVENTS SOIL FROM STICKING TO THE BODY

STRONG BACK LEGS FOR PUSHING DUNG ALONG

FACT FILE

DUNG BEETLE BEHAVIOR

1. DWELLERS
Some dung beetles just dive into poop and stay there.

2. TUNNELERS
Some dung beetles tunnel a nest under the poop and dig upward to snack on it every now and then.

3. ROLLERS
Some dung beetles roll a ball of poop away to a burrow.

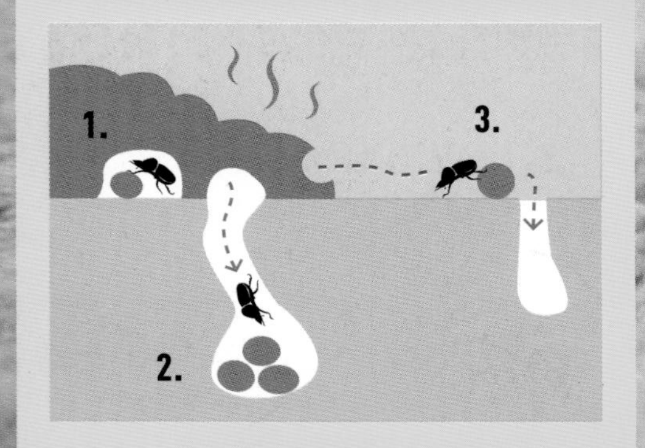

DUNG KING

The ancient Egyptians revered the dung beetle as a symbol of rebirth. One of their sun gods, Khepri, had the head of a dung beetle.

IT'S A RECORD!

The world's strongest insect is the male horned Onthophogus taurus *dung beetle. It uses its strength to push its male rivals away from a female.*

Here's how it compares with other animals:

DUNG BEETLE—can lift 1,141 times its own body weight (the equivalent of a human lifting six school buses).

LEAFCUTTER ANT—can lift 50 times its own body weight.

MALE GORILLA—can lift 10 times its own body weight.

STRONGEST HUMAN—can lift 2.3 times his own body weight.

MALE AFRICAN ELEPHANT—can lift 1.7 times its own body weight.

A species of **South American dung beetle** rides on the back of snails and eats the snail poop.

2 MONTHS

The length of time some female dung beetles look after their young, making them the best insect mothers in the animal kingdom.

Dung beetles navigate poop balls to their burrows using the Sun, the Moon, and even the Milky Way. Scientists discovered this by putting tiny hats on dung beetles to block their sight.

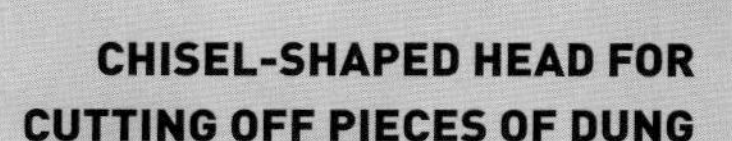

CHISEL-SHAPED HEAD FOR CUTTING OFF PIECES OF DUNG

STRONG FRONT LEGS FOR DIGGING, SHAPING POOP, AND FIGHTING (IF MALE)

The dung beetles find poop by smell or by hanging around pooping creatures (sometimes hooked to the fur around the back, waiting for poop to come out).

JUMP CHAMP

The flea is a minibeast jumping supremo that can leap about 200 times its own body length. It also has a dark side that sucks . . . literally! It sucks up blood from mammals and birds through its tubelike mouth parts.

CAT FLEA

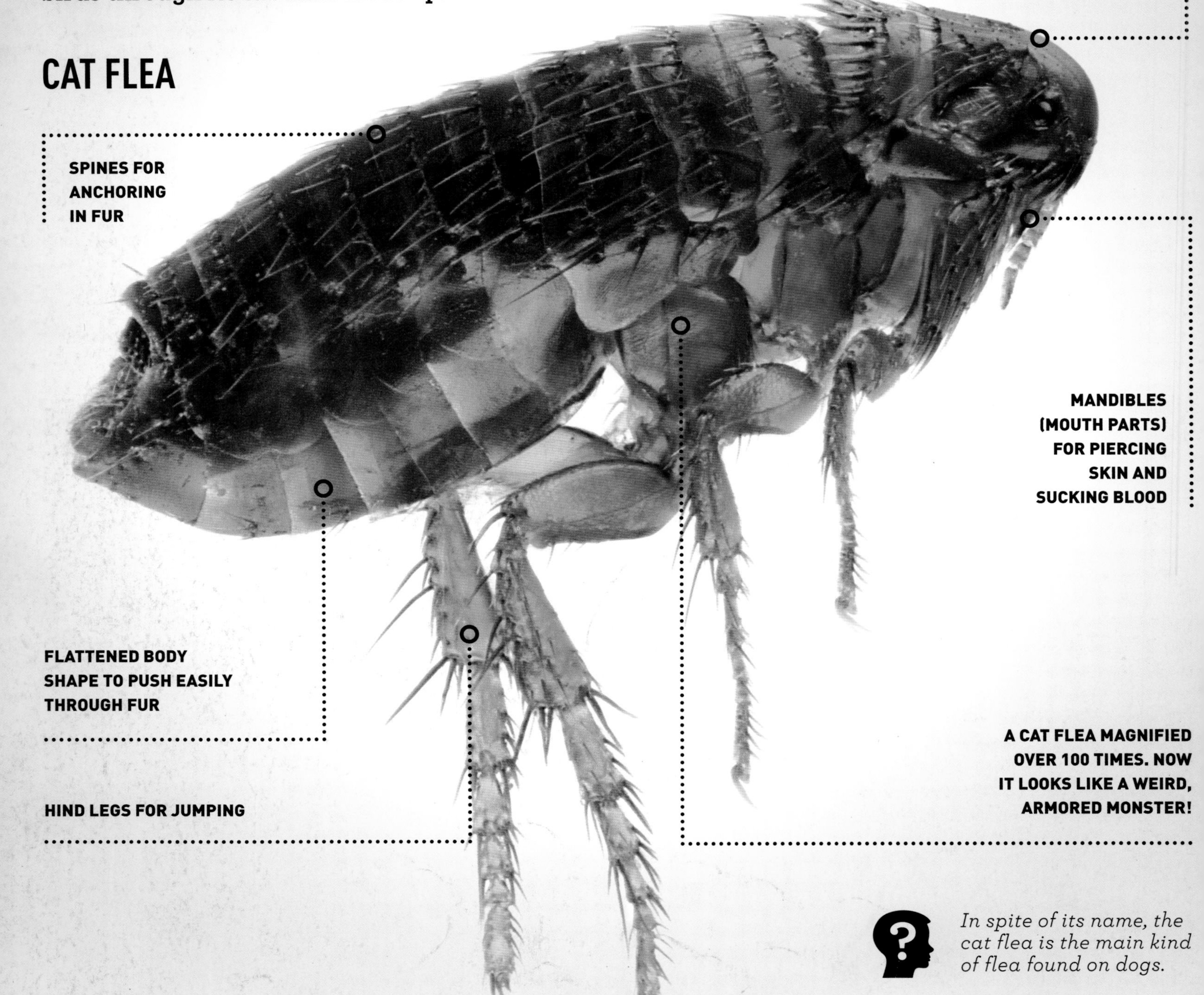

A CAT FLEA MAGNIFIED OVER 100 TIMES. NOW IT LOOKS LIKE A WEIRD, ARMORED MONSTER!

In spite of its name, the cat flea is the main kind of flea found on dogs.

SUCKING CYCLE

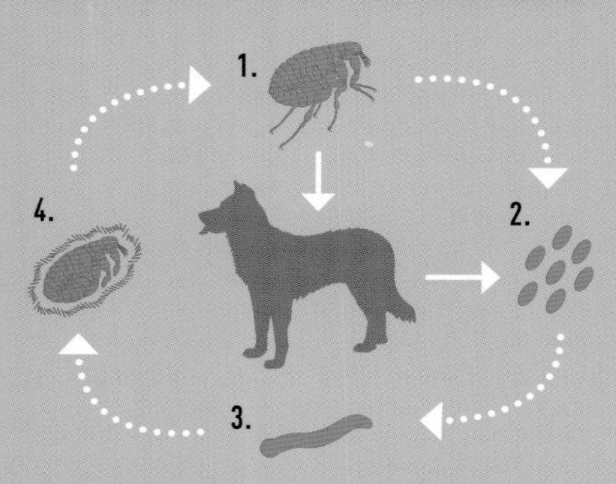

1. Pet fleas jump onto a cat or dog and suck the animal's blood. The females lay eggs on its skin.

2. The eggs drop off onto carpets.

3. Tiny larvae hatch out.

4. The larvae develop into fleas and jump onto any passing pet, ready to begin sucking at Step 1.

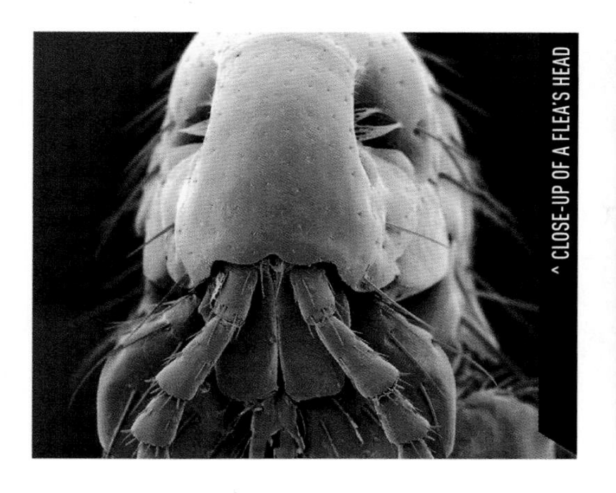

^ CLOSE-UP OF A FLEA'S HEAD

FLEA POWER!

- An average cat flea (0.07 in. long) can leap vertically up to 7.8 in. and horizontally up to 15.7 in.
- Multiply your height by 100 to see how far you'd leap vertically if you had flea power.
- Multiply your height by 200 to find out how far you'd get horizontally.

2,000

There are more than 2,000 different species of flea around the world.

30,000 x

Fleas can jump up to 30,000 times without resting.

If you could jump like a flea, you could jump over the Pyramid of Giza!

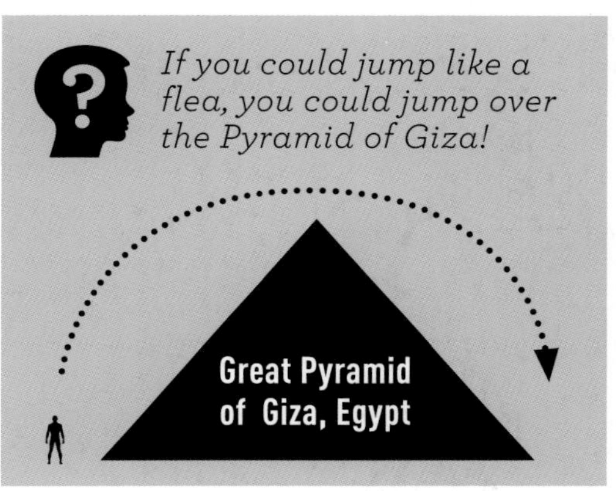

A female flea can lay 30–40 eggs a day.

JURASSIC FLEA

In Jurassic dinosaur times there were giant fleas about ten times the size of today's cat fleas.

GIDDY UP!

Fleas can move objects up to 20,000 times their own body weight. Flea circuses use fleas to perform acts of strength, such as pulling tiny carriages.

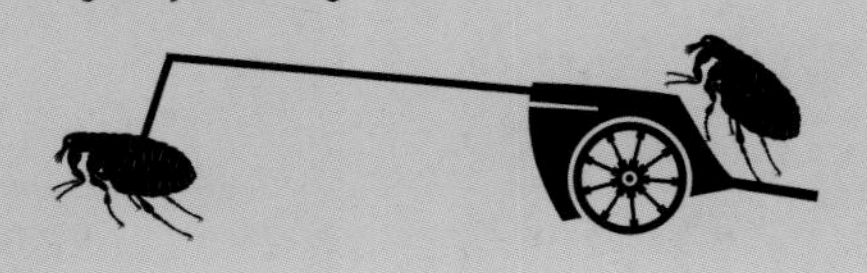

50 x

When a flea jumps, it can accelerate at 6.23 ft. per sec.—around 50 times faster than the US Space Shuttle accelerates after lift off.

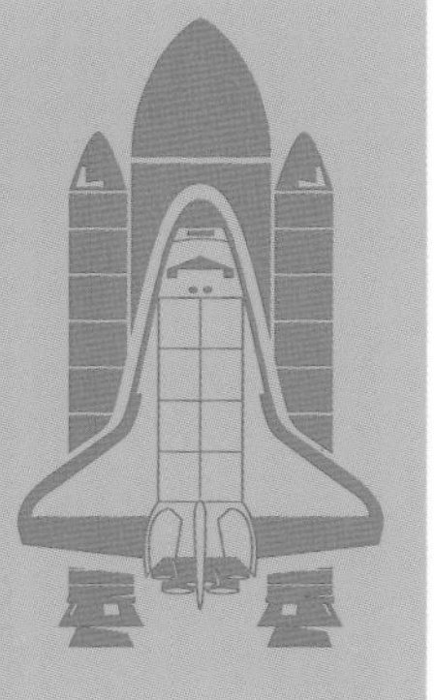

BEST BUG BUILDERS

There are around 2,000 types of termites, tiny see-through insects that live together in colonies. Some termites are mound-builders. They make towering nests using mud mixed with their spit!

The termites constantly exchange a mixture of food and spit with each other. They eat each other's poop, too.

TERMITE MOUND

FACT FILE

INSIDE A TERMITE MOUND

1. Small channels and wide central chimneys provide air-conditioning in the nest.

2. Air circulates around the nest. Heat leaves through the outer walls, and oxygen comes in.

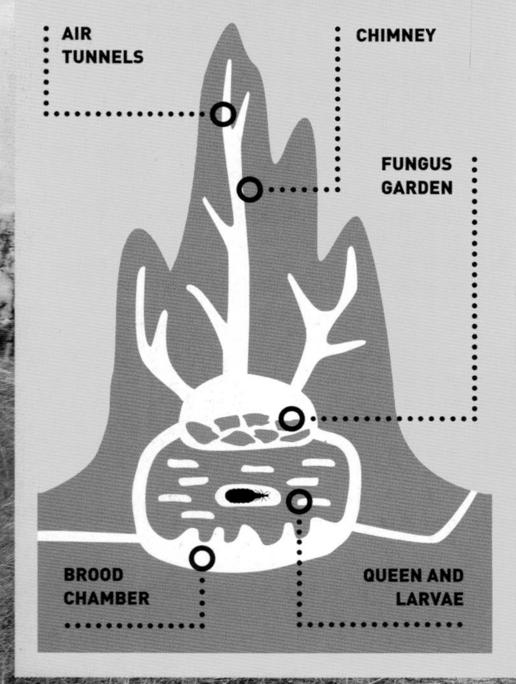

ROYAL *RULE*

Termite nests are highly organized, with soldiers to defend them and workers to feed and look after a queen and king. The king mates with the queen, who spends her whole life (up to 15 years) laying eggs.

HEADBANGING *GLUE GUNS*

Soldier termites try to stop ant attackers by shooting sticky glue from their snouts.

When a nest is attacked the soldiers bang their heads against the nest wall, sending warning vibrations round the nest.

^ TERMITE QUEEN

The number of eggs laid by a termite queen. Her abdomen grows so fat with eggs that it looks like a white sausage and is the size of a human finger.

IT'S A RECORD!

42 FEET HIGH

The height of the world's tallest termite mound. It was found in the Democratic Republic of Congo, Africa.

2 MILLION+

The number of mound-building termites living in one nest.

WORKER SOLDIER

^ TERMITE WORKERS

550 *lb.* OF SOIL

The average amount of soil that mound-building termites move each year.

Secret Recipe

The mound-building termites collect leaves and chew them up to make compost inside the nest. They add fungus, which grows into a thick mesh and turns the compost crumbly—food for the termites.

TASTY *TERMITES*

Some creatures try to break into nests to eat termites. Aardvarks will rip at a nest with long claws.

An aardvark has a sticky tongue up to 12 in. long, which it sticks into the tunnels of a termite nest once it breaks one open.

MAKE SOME NOISE

Some insects may be small, but they're super loud! Crickets, cicadas, and katydids can all fill the air with sound—and cicadas hold the insect record for noisiness.

CICADA

CICADAS MEASURE UP TO 2.25 IN., DEPENDING ON THE SPECIES

CICADAS CALL DURING THE HOTTEST HOURS OF THE DAY

MALE CICADAS MAKE A NOISE TO ATTRACT MATES OR TO WARN OFF OTHER MALES

ALTHOUGH EACH CICADA MAKES A CLICKING SOUND, WHEN LOTS OF MALE CICADAS CALL TOGETHER, IT MAKES A LOUD, CONTINUOUS HUM

CICADAS ARE FOUND ALL OVER THE WORLD, EXCEPT IN ANTARCTICA. THERE ARE AROUND 3,000 DIFFERENT SPECIES.

FACT FILE

HOW CICADAS MAKE A NOISE

To make a clicking noise, the male cicada flexes the tiny drumlike tymbal organs on its abdomen. The almost hollow abdomen amplifies the noise (makes it louder).

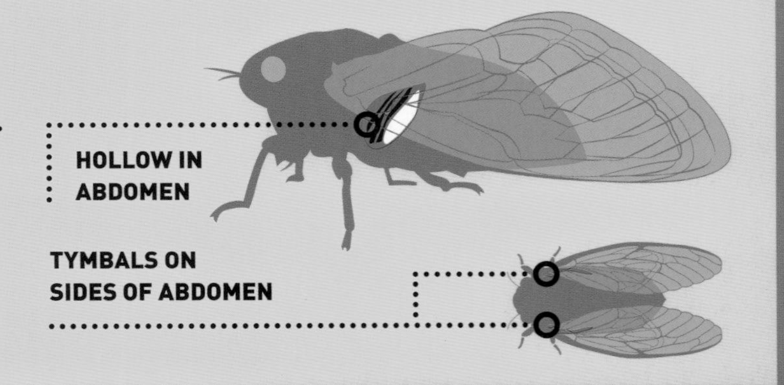

In China, baby cicadas are deep-fried and eaten.

WHO'S *KEEPING YOU UP?*

Crickets and katydids call at night. Cicadas call during the day.

^ CRICKET

LOUDEST BUGS

EUROPEAN MOLE CRICKET
96 decibels at 20 in. away

AFRICAN CICADA
106.7 decibels at 20 in. away

WALKER'S CICADA
108.9 decibels at 20 in. away

These noise levels are the equivalent of standing right next to a jackhammer or a loud rock band.

^ KATYDID

BODY POPPERS

Crickets and katydids make noise by scraping the top of one forewing against the underside of the other wing. The underside has toothlike peg structures. Making noise using body parts is called stridulation.

BELOW 55°F

When it gets this cold, crickets will stop singing.

IT'S A RECORD!

NOISE *RECORD*

For its body size of about 0.07 in. (about as big as a grain of rice), the male Micronecta scholtzi *(water boatman beetle) makes the loudest noise of any insect. It sings at 99 decibels.*

NOT *LISTENING!*

The male cicada must stop its ear structures from working while it calls. Otherwise it would deafen itself!

^ BESS BEETLE

14 The number of different sounds **bess beetles** (a family of beetles living in hot countries) can make. They live in rotting logs, so they rub their body parts to communicate with each other in the darkness.

SEEING IS BELIEVING

Insects don't have the same kind of eyes as humans. If they did, their eyes would need to be so big they would take up most of their head. Instead, most have compound eyes, which have lots of little lenses.

Flies don't have pupils to control the amount of light that comes into their eye. Instead, they have internal eye cells that absorb excess light so that they don't get dazzled.

INSECTS HAVE COMPOUND EYES, SIMPLE EYES, OR COMBINATIONS OF THE TWO, WHEREAS FLIES HAVE BOTH

ROBBER FLY

A COMPOUND EYE IS MADE UP OF THOUSANDS OF OMMATIDIA. EACH OMMATIDIUM IS A TINY EYE—A LENS LEADING DOWN TO A NERVE.

FLIES CAN'T FOCUS SHARPLY, SO THEY ARE SHORT-SIGHTED

FLIES MIGHT NOT SEE ALL THAT CLEARLY, BUT THEY ARE AMAZING AT SPOTTING WHEN SOMETHING MOVES NEARBY. THAT'S WHY THEY ARE SO HARD TO CATCH!

THE OMMATIDIUM LENSES GATHER LIGHT. CELLS IN THE OMMATIDIUM SENSE THE LIGHT AND SEND INFORMATION ABOUT IT TO THE NERVE. THE NERVE RELAYS THE INFORMATION TO THE BRAIN.

FLIES CAN'T MOVE THEIR EYES AROUND LIKE HUMANS. INSTEAD, THEY HAVE BIG BULGING EYES THAT CAN SEE ALMOST 360° ALL AROUND THE FLY.

5 EYES

As well as two compound eyes, flies have three tiny simple eyes on their forehead.

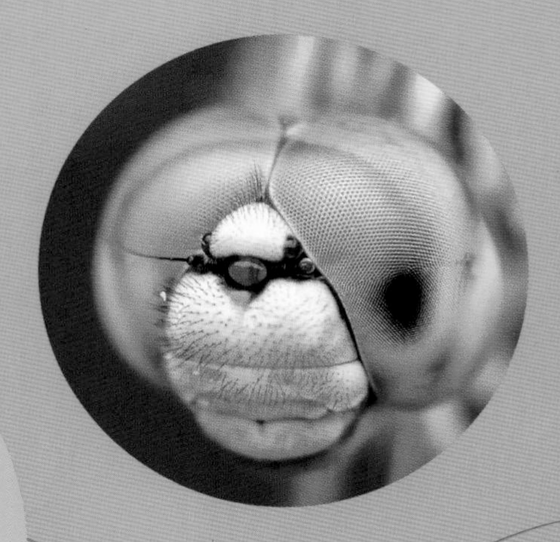

UP TO 30,000

The number of individual lenses in the compound eye of a dragonfly. Their super sight helps them to fly acrobatically.

Scientists made a tiny pair of glasses for a praying mantis, just 0.2 in. wide. They stuck them on with beeswax and showed the mantis a 3-D movie of flies to see how good its 3-D sight was. It's the only insect with 3-D sight (see pg. 48 for more).

The picture seen by an insect is like a computer image made up of big pixels, combining to make one blurry image (right). That's what most flies see.

1 *vs.* 100

Cockroaches are more sensitive to light than any other creature. They can sense a single photon—just one tiny particle of light. Humans can't see any amount of light below 100 photons.

WRONG FOR RED

Insects don't have the eye cells to see all the colors we can. They can't see red, for instance.

RIGHT FOR NIGHT

The eyes of night-flying insects are much better at gathering light than day-flying insects. The night-fliers can see using low levels of moonlight or starlight.

BUGS AROUND THE HOUSE

There's something you should know. You're sharing your home with bugs, and you're eating them, too! But there's no need to freak out. They're not hurting you, although it's possible they could be eating your stuff.

CARPENTER BEES

These bees bore into wood to make tunnels. They overwinter in the tunnels and lay their eggs there in spring. An infestation of carpenter bees can make wooden sections of a house collapse. Their poop stains the walls, too.

THRIPS

These slender little insects love to eat cereal. You might find them lurking in old cereal packets or flour bags that are past their freshness date.

SILVERFISH

These silvery wingless insects eat starch—for example wallpaper paste—fabrics, and cereal. They hide in damp locations such as the bathroom, the basement, or the kitchen. Then they wriggle out at night, looking for food.

400 MILLION YEARS

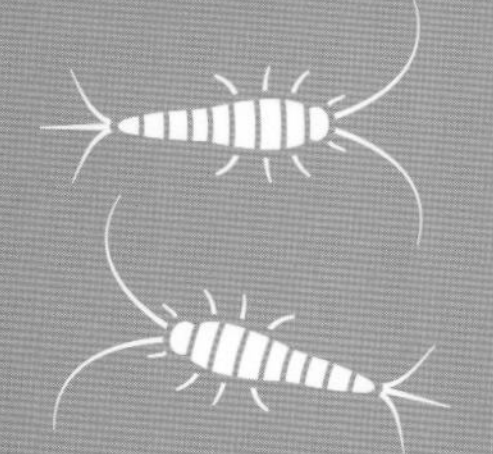

Silverfish have been around on Earth for 400 million years. They appeared 100 million years before the dinosaurs.

WOOD-EATING BEETLES

There are several different kinds. The deathwatch beetle is the noisiest. It bangs its head against wood at night, making a ticking noise to signal to other beetles.

INSECTS ON YOUR PLATE

Everybody eats bits and pieces of insects without knowing it. Tiny insects such as aphids and thrips feed on plant crops and get accidentally harvested along with the plants. They make it into food when the crops are made into processed food. They don't do any harm, and the pieces are too small to see.

1–2 *LB.*

The average person is estimated to eat 1–2 lb. of flies, maggots, and other bug fragments each year.

In many countries there are lawful limits to the number of bug fragments that can be sold in food. Here are some examples of US limits:

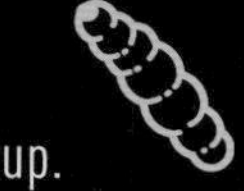

CANNED SPINACH
No more than **50 APHIDS** or **THRIPS** per 3.5 oz.

CANNED FRUIT JUICE
No more than **1 MAGGOT** per cup.

CHOCOLATE
No more than **60 INSECT** fragments per 3.5 oz.

PEANUT BUTTER
No more than **30 INSECT** fragments per 3.5 oz.

TERMITES

Termites can nest under homes and quickly chomp through the floor joists and roof beams. An average termite colony eats nearly 13 lb. of wood a year. That would be quite a few floor joists or roof beams!

DON'T COUNT!

The deathwatch beetle gets its name because legend has it that the ticking noise it makes at night is counting down to someone's death!

Tiny dust mites live in our homes, too. They're not insects, though. They're arachnids, as are spiders.

A BAD CROWD

Swarms of locusts have been feared for centuries. No other insects can do as much damage to crops as quickly, sometimes leading to deadly food shortages.

LOCUST SWARM

THE LOCUST'S BACK LEGS ARE STRONG FOR JUMPING

DESERT LOCUSTS GROW 2–2.5 IN. LONG

MOUTHPARTS FOR CHEWING UP PLANTS

THERE ARE A DOZEN OR SO SPECIES OF SWARMING LOCUSTS. DESERT LOCUSTS SWARM THE MOST. THEY LIVE IN AFRICA, THE MIDDLE EAST, AND ASIA.

FINE, SENSITIVE HAIRS ON THE LOCUST'S BODY HELP IT TO DETECT AIR MOVEMENT AROUND IT

A SWARM CAN TRAVEL LONG DISTANCES, EVEN ACROSS OCEANS!

AS THEY TRAVEL THEY LAND TO EAT, STRIPPING PLANTS IN RECORD TIME

40-80 MILLION *PER SQ. MILE*

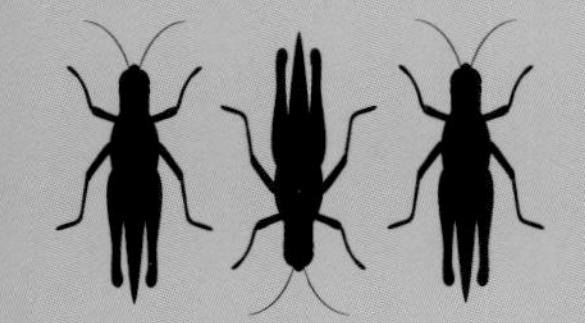

The number of locusts in a big swarm of one square mile.

^ HEAD OF A LOCUST

Rainfall can cause an explosion in locust numbers. Soon there is not enough plant food for all the locusts to eat. Then they swarm and travel to new areas, looking for food.

IT'S A RECORD!

460 SQUARE MILES

The approximate size of the biggest locust swarm ever recorded.

SWARM STUFF

Scientists have discovered that the trigger for a locust swarm is a body chemical called serotonin. Locusts about to swarm have increased serotonin levels. Controlling their serotonin could be a way to control swarming.

HOW TO COOK A LOCUST

In parts of Asia and Africa, locusts are caught in nets and cooked as a protein-rich crunchy snack. Here are two cooking methods:

FROM SWAZILAND

Roast the locusts on a fire. Eat the roast legs (they're the tastiest part), and then grind the rest of the locust into a powder to sprinkle on food.

FROM CAMBODIA

Slit open a locust and stuff it with peanuts. Grill in a wok.

1 TON OF LOCUSTS (only a small part of a swarm) could eat the same amount of food in one day as:

10 ELEPHANTS

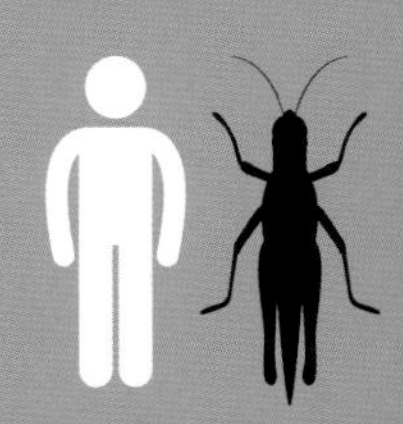

25 CAMELS

2,500 HUMANS

^ SWARM OF LOCUSTS

400 MILLION *LB.*

Each locust can eat its own weight in plants each day—about 0.07 ounces. A big swarm could eat over 400 million lb. of plants in just one day.

EAR HERE!

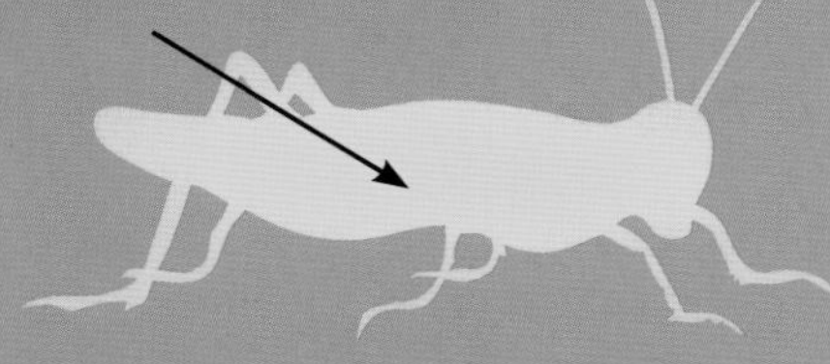

Locusts have their ears on their abdomens.

IT'S A SMELLY WORLD!

Smell is a big part of the life of most insects. It's used to find food, friends, homes, and even to trick unwary prey. Yet insects don't have noses!

FACT FILE

HOW DO INSECTS SMELL?

- When a smell molecule (a particle of smell) reaches an insect, it enters a special body part called a sensing organ, usually located on the insect's antenna.
- The sensing organ triggers a signal in the insect's nervous system. The signal "tells" the insect what to do—making it fly toward a mate, for example.

40+

The number of different chemicals in a bee alarm pheromone, which is released when the bee stings.

ALL ABOUT SMELL

Insects make a group of smelly chemicals called pheromones. The smells act as signals that other insects can recognize. Pheromones are as complicated and subtle as the finest perfumes.

EACH COLONY HAS ITS OWN SMELL. BEES FROM OTHER COLONIES WON'T BE ALLOWED IN.

IF A COLONY OF BEES SWARMS (LEAVES THE HIVE), THE QUEEN'S PHEROMONE KEEPS THE BEES TOGETHER AS THEY FOLLOW HER

PHEROMONES ARE VITAL FOR COLONY INSECTS SUCH AS BEES, ANTS, AND WASPS. THE SMELLS HELP KEEP THE COLONY WORKING TOGETHER.

BEE WORKERS MARK FOOD SOURCES WITH PHEROMONES AS A SIGNAL TO OTHER BEES IN THEIR COLONY

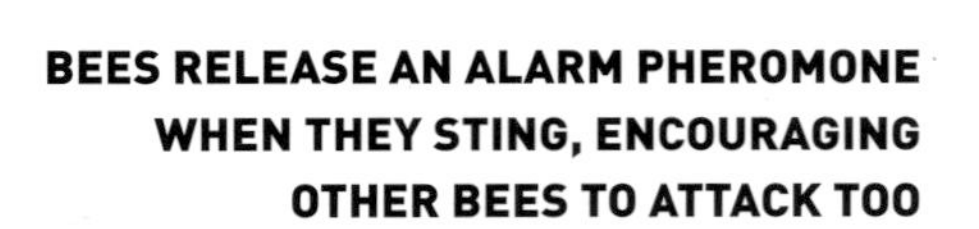

BEES RELEASE AN ALARM PHEROMONE WHEN THEY STING, ENCOURAGING OTHER BEES TO ATTACK TOO

INSIDE A HIVE, THE QUEEN BEE SECRETES A PHEROMONE THAT THE WORKER BEES PASS AROUND TO EACH OTHER. IT CONTROLS THEM, STOPPING THEM FROM DEVELOPING INTO QUEENS THEMSELVES.

7 MILES

The male **emperor moth** can smell a female up to 7 miles away.

^ EMPEROR MOTH

^ MEALWORM BEETLE

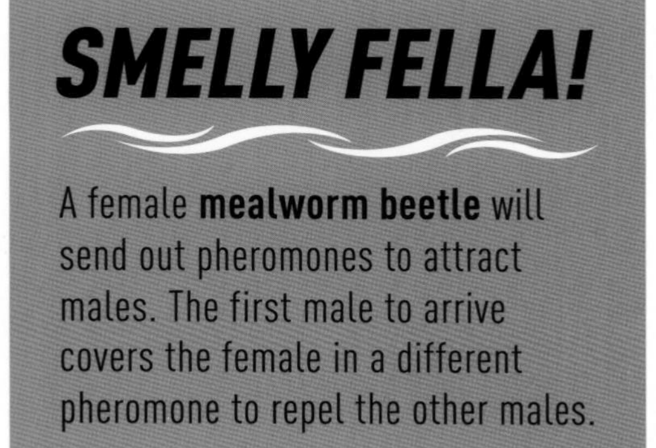

SMELLY FELLA!

A female **mealworm beetle** will send out pheromones to attract males. The first male to arrive covers the female in a different pheromone to repel the other males.

Beekeepers use smoke to mask bee pheromone alarm signals, calming down the bees so the beekeepers can approach.

SMELL *SNEAK*

Bolas spiders can fake the pheromone of a female night-flying moth. When the male moth arrives, it gets eaten.

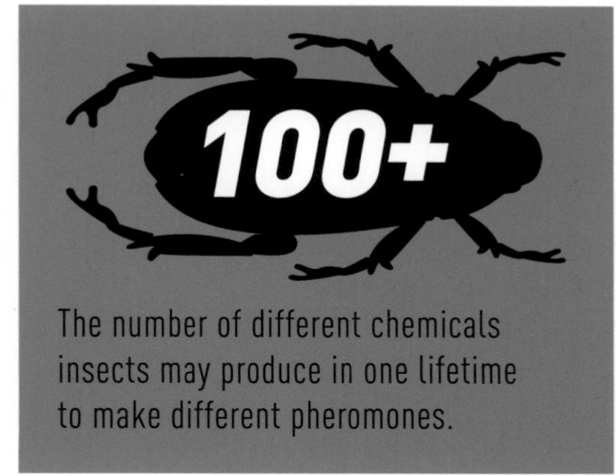

The number of different chemicals insects may produce in one lifetime to make different pheromones.

PEACEKEEPER

To mix two bee colonies, beekeepers must use techniques to gradually mingle the two different colony pheromones. Otherwise, the bees will fight.

^ COTTON CROPS

MOTH REPELLENT

Beet armyworms are pesky moths that can destroy cotton crops. By spraying female pheromones over the fields, farmers can make it difficult for the males to find females and mate, helping to cut down the population.

DEADLY IS THE FEMALE

Mosquitoes are the deadliest insects as far as humans are concerned. They are responsible for over a million deaths a year, mainly in Africa, through passing on fatal diseases such as malaria.

FACT FILE

1. When a female mosquito bites, it stabs two tubes into the skin.

2. One tube injects an enzyme (chemical) that stop the blood from clotting.

3. The other tube sucks up the blood.

MOSQUITOES

Mosquitoes find their warm-blooded hosts by detecting:

- **Body warmth**
- **Carbon dioxide breathed out by the host**
- **Smell *(eg: chemicals in sweat)***
- **Movement**

Mosquitoes actually prefer the blood of horses, birds, and cattle to human blood.

A MOSQUITO CAN DRINK UP TO THREE TIMES ITS OWN WEIGHT IN BLOOD

FEMALE MOSQUITOES BEAT THEIR WINGS 500 TIMES A SECOND, MAKING THE HUMMING NOISE YOU CAN HEAR WHEN THEY ARRIVE

HEAT SENSORS ON THE MOUTHPARTS CAN DETECT WARM BLOOD CAPILLARIES ON THE BODY OF THE VICTIM

ONLY FEMALES HAVE THE MOUTHPARTS FOR SUCKING BLOOD

FEMALES DON'T FEED ON BLOOD THEMSELVES. THEY USE IT TO SUPPLY THEIR EGGS WITH FOOD

MOSQUITOES LAY UP TO 300 EGGS AT A TIME (IN STAGNANT WATER) EVERY THREE DAYS

3,500+

The number of mosquito species in the world.

Mosquito bites swell up and itch because of an allergic reaction to the mosquito's saliva.

ENEMY *INSECTS*

Here are some other insects that can pass on diseases to humans:

TSETSE FLY
Carrier of sleeping sickness, which kills thousands in Africa every year.

BOT FLY
Lays its larvae under the skin.

KISSING BUG *(BELOW)*
Named because it bites the lips of its human victims when they are asleep. It passes on Chagas disease.

THE FROZEN FEW

Mosquitoes die or hibernate in winter. Some lay their eggs in freezing water before dying. The eggs are preserved, frozen until spring.

Mosquito larvae are called wrigglers (below). They live in water before becoming adults.

KILLER *BUGS*

Three species are responsible for passing on deadly diseases in Africa:

ANOPHELES—malaria
CULEX—encephalitis
AEDES—yellow fever, dengue fever

^ MOSQUITO LARVAE

Some famous malaria sufferers:

John F. Kennedy
Mother Teresa
Genghis Khan
Christopher Columbus *(right)*

Mosquito is Spanish for "little fly."

79 MILLION *YEARS AGO*

Mosquitoes were around in Cretaceous times, along with dinosaurs. In the plot of the movie *Jurassic Park*, dinosaurs were cloned from blood found in ancient mosquitoes preserved in amber (below), though this isn't possible in real life!

Mosquitoes love the smell of sweat, body lotions, and perfume. They don't like a chemical called DEET or lemon-eucalyptus oil. These are used in repellents.

IT'S A RECORD!

SPACE *BUG*

A mosquito survived for 18 months in space in an experimental container fixed to the outside of the International Space Station.

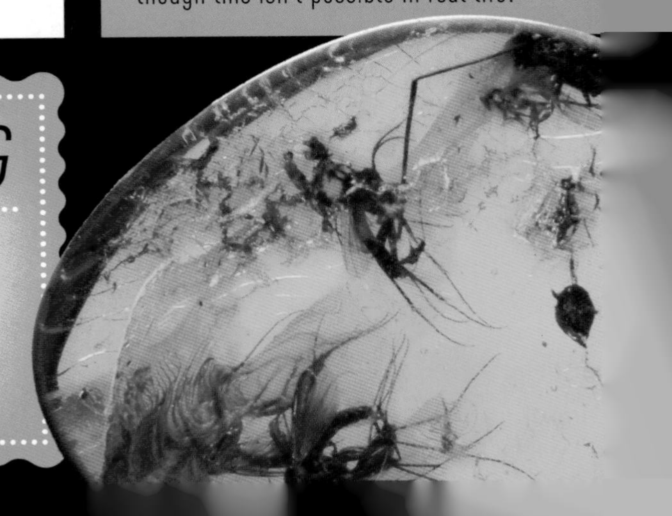

POND PATROL

Ponds may look peaceful, but in fact they are dangerous places! A vicious range of hunting insects lurk beneath the surface, just waiting for a meal.

INSECT YOUNG

Before insects grow into adults, they go through the stage of being a larvae or a nymph. Lots of nymphs and beetle larvae live in ponds, hunting for other creatures to eat. The biggest beetle larvae can even catch small fish.

Great diving beetle larvae are sometimes called water tigers because they are so fierce.

FACT FILE

LARVAE VS. NYMPH

- A larvae is a baby insect that looks completely different than its adult version. Eventually it will metamorphosize (see pg. 18). A nymph only partly changes its shape as it grows.
- Some insects spend their whole lives in water. Some live on land nearby when they become adults.

GREAT DIVING BEETLE LARVAE

- This larvae sinks its large, pointed jaws into prey; it then pumps digestive juices into the prey to liquefy it, and sucks up the "body soup."
- It raises its tail above the water to take in oxygen, breathing in through holes (spiracles) in its body.

DRAGONFLY NYMPH

- This nymph's lower lip has extended hooks on it for catching prey.
- It moves along by expelling mini water jets out of the back of its abdomen.
- It likes to eat mosquito larvae, which makes it useful to humans.

WATER STRIDER NYMPH

- This nymph can walk across water.
- The underside of its body is covered with water-repellent hair.
- It can sense vibrations on the water's surface when a small insect falls in. It rushes over, pushes its mouth into its prey, and sucks out its insides.

UPSIDE-**DOWN**

Backswimmer beetles get their name because they swim on their backs.

Many insect larvae and nymphs are cannibals (they eat their own kind).

CLEVER *LEGS*

Water striders use their legs very efficiently:

FRONT LEGS to catch prey
MIDDLE LEGS to paddle
BACK LEGS to steer and brake

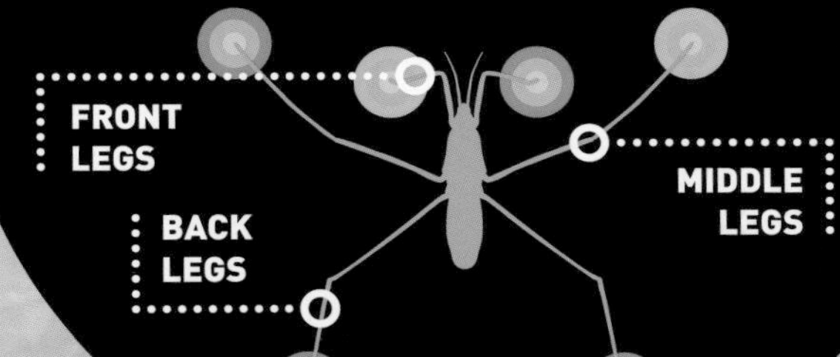

14 MEALS *IN* 6 HOURS

Amount of mosquito larvae hunted and eaten on average by dragonfly larvae (below).

5 YEARS +

Some dragonflies live as larvae for many years before becoming an adult, surviving for just a few weeks.

8 WEEKS

The time it takes for a water strider to grow from an egg to an adult.

NASTY NIPPERS

Some water beetles can give you a painful, though harmless bite.

FAKE ***FLY***

Fishermen try to fool fish by putting yummy-looking fake insects on the end of their fishing line.

IN DISGUISE

Many insects are camouflage experts. They use all sorts of cunning disguises to avoid hungry enemies or to help them stay hidden as they lie in wait for something tasty to come along.

PRAYING MANTIS

The praying mantis is the insect master of disguise and ambush.

PRAYING MANTISES HAVE COMPOUND AND SIMPLE EYES. THEY CAN SEE UP TO 60 FT. AWAY AND HAVE 3-D VISION (SEE PG. 37).

MOUTH PARTS FOR BITING ITS FOOD

FEMALE PRAYING MANTISES SOMETIMES EAT THEIR MALE MATES

STRONG FRONT LEGS FOR GRABBING VICTIMS AT SPEEDS FASTER THAN OUR EYES CAN SEE

THE FRONT LEGS HAVE SPIKES FOR CATCHING VICTIMS

The praying mantis can turn its triangular head 180° to see its surroundings. It's the only insect that can do this.

Praying mantises get their name because they appear to hold up their forelegs in quiet prayer. In fact, they are standing as still as possible, waiting to strike.

TYPES OF INSECT DISGUISE

CAMOUFLAGE

Blending in with surrounding colors and patterns. The praying mantis does this.

COUNTERSHADING

A body that is dark on top and light underneath. From above it blends in with the dark background. From below it blends in with the light. Caterpillars often have this.

AVOIDING A SHADOW

Keeping the body really flat to avoid casting a shadow. Leaf bugs do this.

CRYPSIS

Mimicking an object such as a leaf, stick, or twig. Stick insects are a good example.

BEING ASYMMETRICAL

Having wings that are patterned and shaped differently than each other. Tropical katydids do this so that birds won't recognize them as insects to eat.

^ PRAYING MANTIS

MASTERS OF DISGUISE

THE WALKING FLOWER MANTIS looks like a pretty pink orchid flower.

THE LEAF-LITTER MANTIS looks like a dead leaf.

THE GHOST MANTIS mimics a dying leaf.

THE STICK MANTIS makes a very convincing twig.

2,400

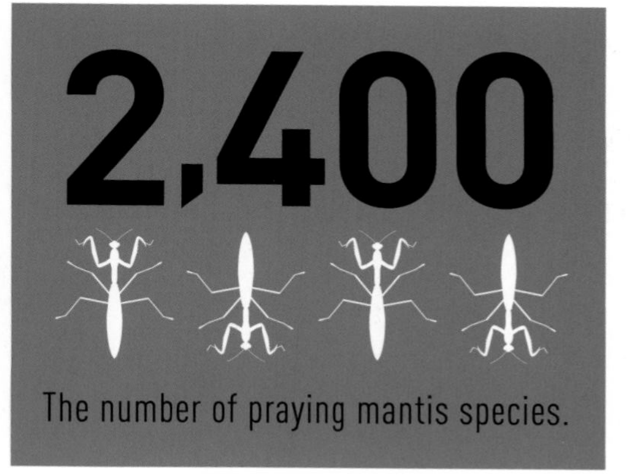

The number of praying mantis species.

^ WALKING FLOWER MANTIS

IT'S A **RECORD!**

7+ *INCHES*

The size of the male African giant stick mantis. That's as long as a very big banana!

The **walking leaf insect** (right) is so cleverly disguised as a leaf that it even has patterns on its wings like the bite marks of caterpillars.

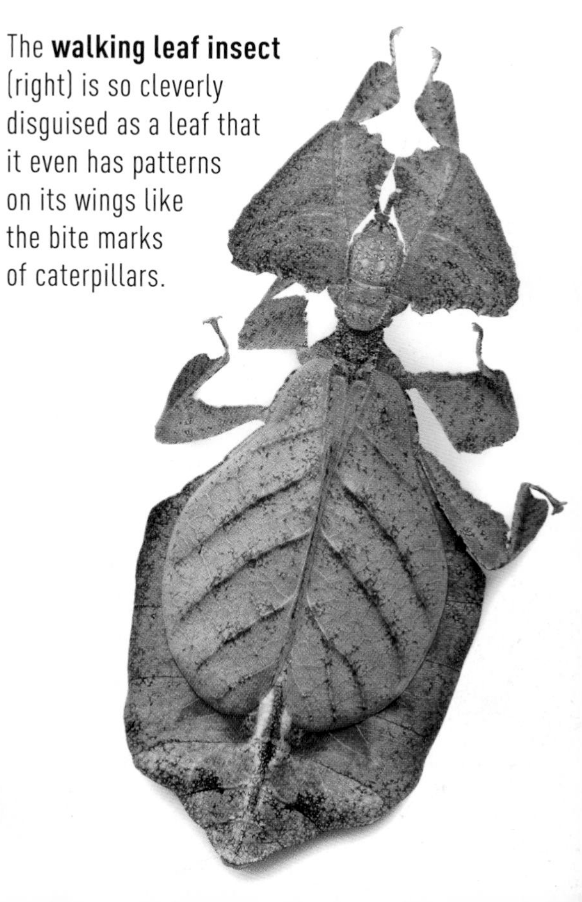

This **lappet moth** caterpillar is camouflaged to blend in with its surroundings to protect it from predators.

Treehoppers win the prize for best small insect disguise. There are species that mimic thorns, leaves, and even other more threatening insects such as wasps and ants.

FLYING ACE

The dragonfly is the acrobatic flying expert of the insect world. It leaves the other flying insects for dead—literally. In fact, it catches them in midair and gobbles them up.

POWERFUL MANDIBLES (JAWS) FOR CHOMPING FOOD

BIG COMPOUND EYES THAT CAN SEE ALMOST 360°

THE DRAGONFLY BREATHES THROUGH SPIRACLES (TINY HOLES) IN ITS ABDOMEN

TWO SETS OF LIGHTWEIGHT, SEE-THROUGH WINGS

DRAGONFLIES ARE SUCH GOOD MIDAIR HUNTERS THAT THEY CATCH 90–95 PERCENT OF THE PREY THEY GO FOR

LONG FRONT LEGS THAT ACT LIKE A BASKET, GRABBING PREY IN MIDAIR

A LONG, THIN, AERODYNAMIC ABDOMEN

CLASPERS AT THE BACK OF THE ABDOMEN FOR MATING AND EGG-LAYING

FACT FILE

- A dragonfly can hover in midair.
- It can also fly straight up and down, and even backward. It does this by controlling its front and back wing sets independently of each other, changing their angle and the number of wing beats to make fantastic aerial maneuvers.

People often mistake the claspers at the back of the dragonfly's body for a stinger. Dragonflies don't sting.

5,000+

The number of dragonfly species, found everywhere except Antarctica.

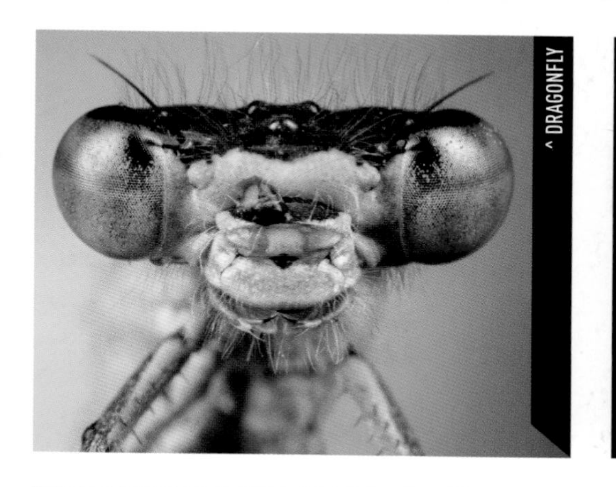
^ DRAGONFLY

NO DENTIST *NEEDED*

Dragonflies and damselflies belong to a group of insects called "odonata," meaning "toothed." But they don't have teeth, only chewing mouthparts.

FAST *FLAPPERS*

The dragonfly is a much more efficient flier than other insects and uses fewer wing beats. Here is a wing-beat comparison.

DRAGONFLY
=30 *WING BEATS A SECOND*

BEE
=200 *WING BEATS A SECOND*

MOSQUITO
=500 *WING BEATS A SECOND*

FLY
=1,000 *WING BEATS A SECOND*

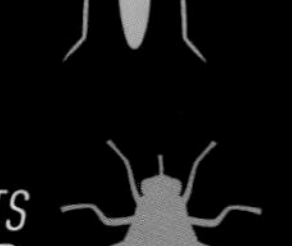

36 MPH

The fastest dragonfly speed recorded so far.

IT'S A RECORD!

7.5 *INCHES*

The wingspan of the biggest example in the dragonfly family: the Megaloprepus caenilatis *damselfly. It flies around Central and South America.*

Dragonflies will eat almost any insect they can catch, but especially mosquitoes.

30–100

The number of mosquitoes an adult dragonfly can munch in one day.

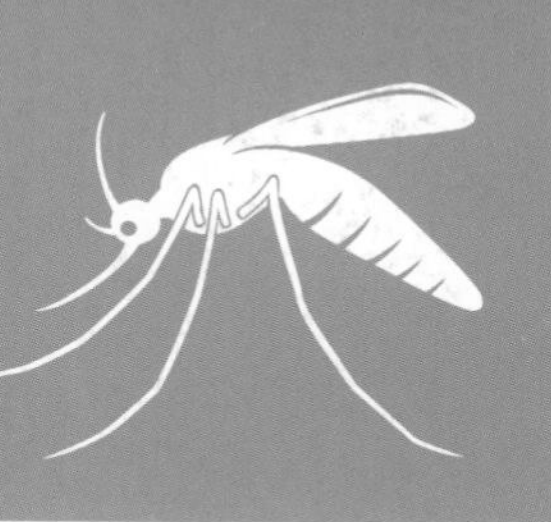

BE GOOD, NOW...

Dragonflies were once called "the devil's darning needle." In legend, they were said to sew up the mouths of naughty children!

2 FEET

Fossils show huge prehistoric dragonflies with wingspans over 2 ft. long.

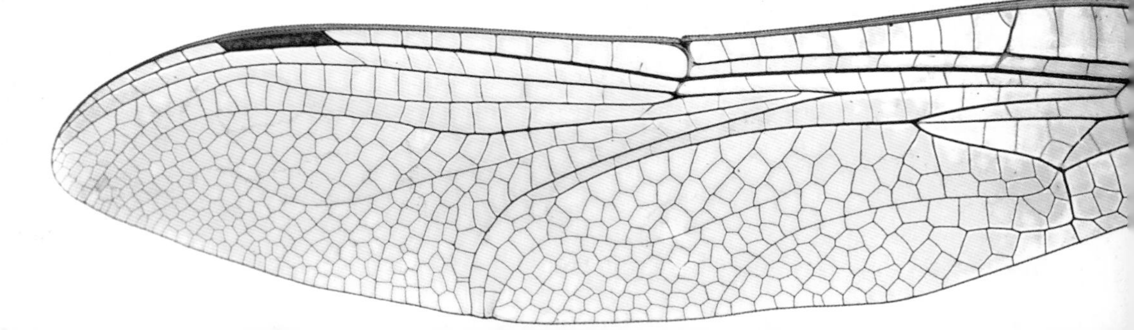

LIGHTING THE WAY

Some insects, such as fireflies, talk to each other using light. That sounds lovely, doesn't it? But don't say "aaah" too soon. A few insects use light to kill!

PYRALIS FIREFLY

The most common North American firefly is the pyralis, also called the lightning bug.

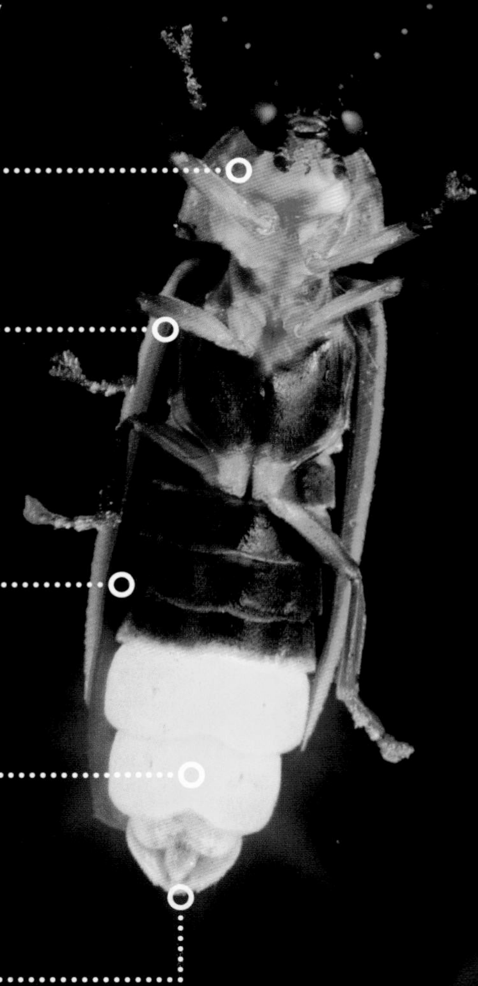

IN MOST FIREFLY SPECIES, MALES AND FEMALES FLASH THEIR LIGHTS TO ATTRACT EACH OTHER. THE MALES FLY AROUND FLASHING, BUT THE FEMALES TEND TO PERCH IN THE TREES OR BUSHES.

PYRALIS FIREFLIES GROW TO AROUND 0.75 IN. LONG

FIREFLY LIGHT IS INCREDIBLY EFFICIENT. IT DOESN'T LOSE ANY ENERGY IN HEAT. A TYPICAL LIGHT BULB LOSES MOST OF ITS ENERGY IN HEAT.

THE GLOWING CHEMICAL INSIDE THE FIREFLIES—LUCIFERIN—IS HEAT-RESISTANT

MALE PYRALIS FIREFLIES FLASH EVERY 5 SECONDS, AND THE FEMALES FLASH EVERY 2 SECONDS

FACT FILE

HOW DO FIREFLIES GLOW?

1. A firefly takes oxygen into special body cells under its abdomen.

2. The oxygen combines with a chemical called luciferin. The luciferin creates light, but not heat.

1/40TH

Firefly light is around one-fortieth the brightness of a candle.

2,000

Number of firefly species in the world.

Fireflies aren't flies. They're actually beetles. They are sometimes called glowworms, too. Different species of fireflies can glow yellow, red, green, or orange.

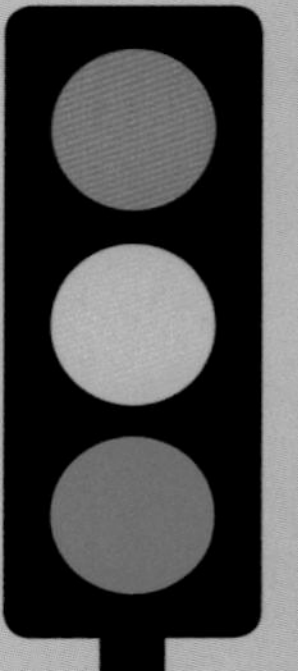

MYSTERY **FLASH**

Scientists are working to create LED lighting and genetically-modified glowing plants using luciferin—the chemical that makes fireflies glow. The idea is for the plants to glow in the dark, lighting up our homes.

DEADLY TRICKSTERS

Female **photuris fireflies** imitate the flashes of a different female firefly species to lure in their males, then eat them!

^ GREAT SMOKY MOUNTAINS

BEETLE **GLOW**

Some **click beetles** have glowing spots. The glow comes from bacteria living under the beetles' exoskeletons.

5 SECONDS *TO LIGHT SHOW*

A few rare locations are home to firefly species that all flash in sync (at the same time). One of these sparkly spots is in the Great Smoky Mountains National Park *(above)*, where the forest floor lights up every 5–8 seconds at certain times of the year.

100 *FEET*

Amazingly, some click beetle lights can be seen up to 100 ft. away in the dark.

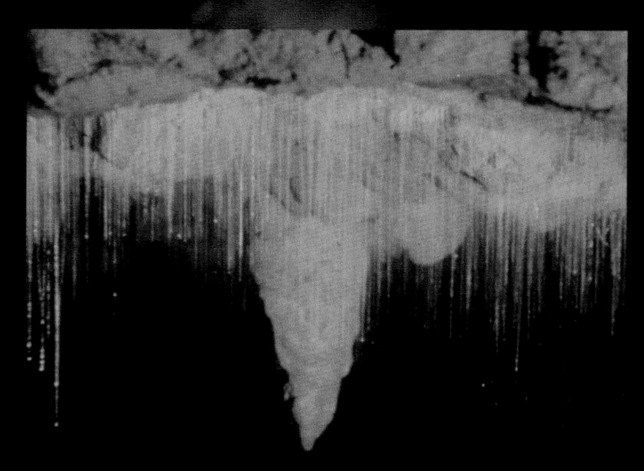

Railroad worms, found in North and South America, are beetles. They have green lights on their body and red lights on their head.

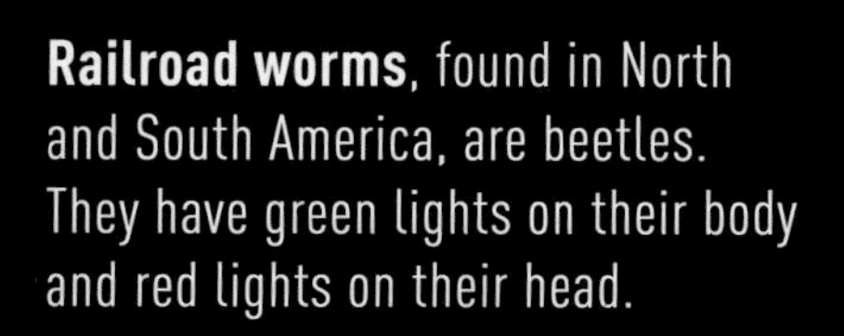

Lucihormetica luckae was an incredibly rare type of glowing cockroach discovered living on an active volcano in Ecuador. We say "was" because the volcano erupted in 2010, so this species may no longer exist. Scientists are still looking.

CAVE CATCHING

In Waitomo Caves, New Zealand, the larvae of the **fungus gnat** glow a magical blue to attract other insects as prey. The prey gets caught on sticky lines of silk dangled by the larvae.

FIRE!

Lots of insects can make poisonous chemicals as a clever defense against danger, but none of them can match the bombardier beetle—the insect chemical lab star.

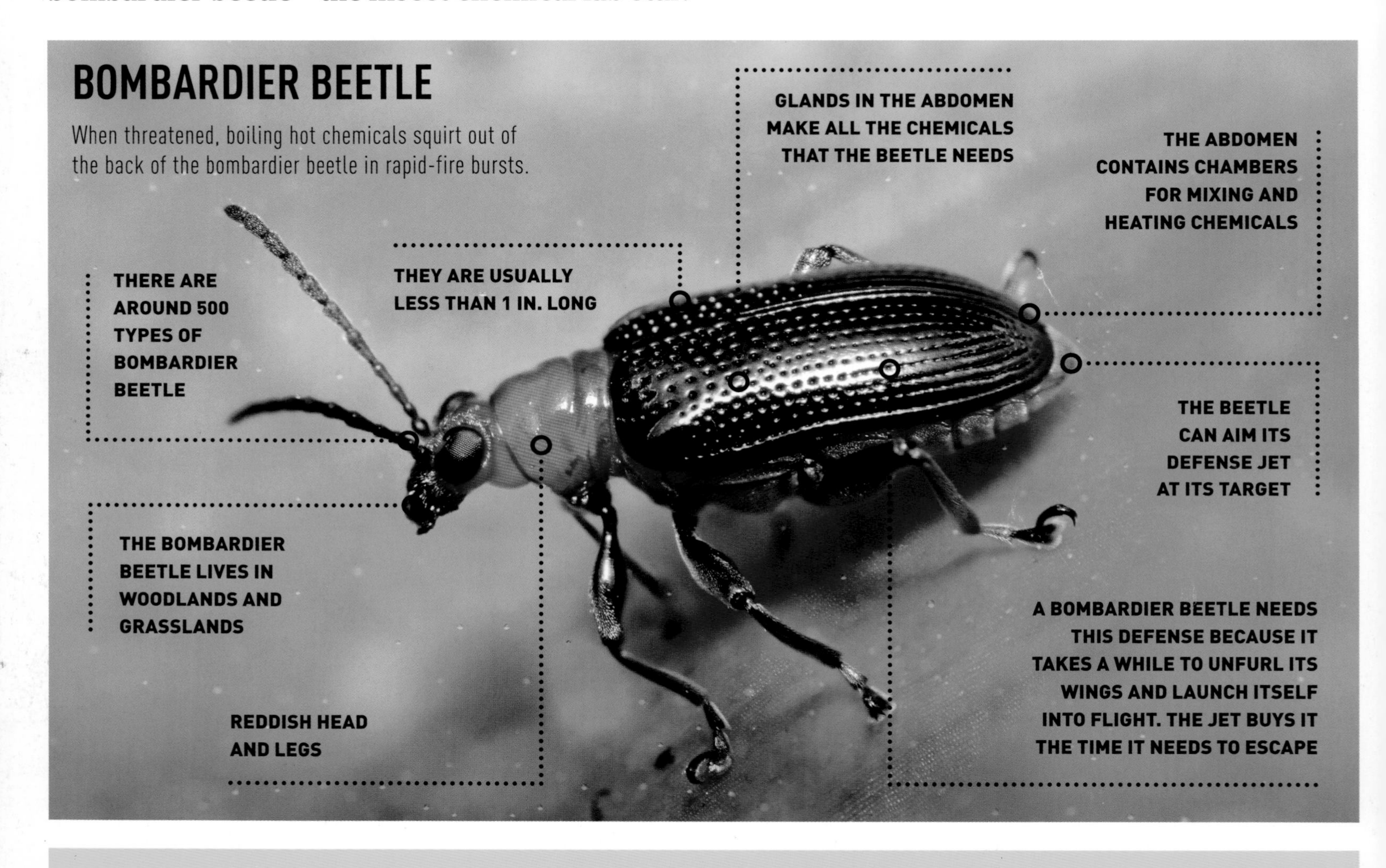

FACT FILE

HOW TO FIRE CHEMICALS

1. Inside the bombardier beetle's abdomen there are two chambers. Chemicals are mixed in the first chamber, then sent into the second chamber.

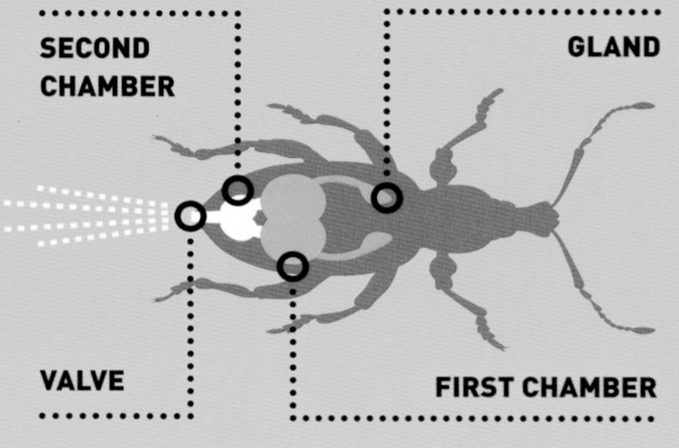

2. In the second chamber they are mixed with an enzyme that superheats them. The chamber is made of reinforced material that withstands the heat and pressure of the chemical cook-up.

3. The boiling chemicals shoot out of a valve at the back of the beetle. The chamber cools slightly (helping to save the beetle from internal harm), and the process repeats.

212°F

The temperature of the bombardier beetle's boiling chemical defense jet.

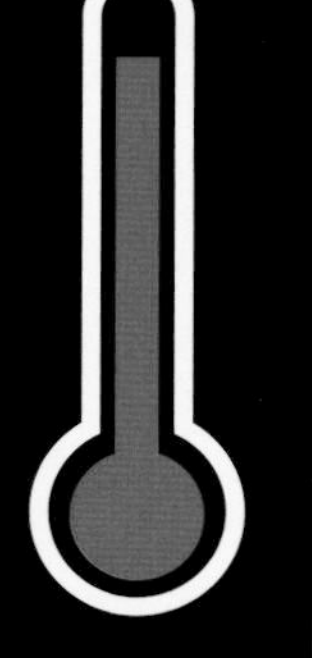

STUCK *DOWN*

Chrysomelid beetles exude sticky chemicals from tiny hairs on their feet if attacked. They glue themselves down, so their enemy can't snatch them up.

STICK *WITH ME*

Staphylinid beetles secrete a glue to gum up the mouths of attackers.

20 *TIMES*

The bombardier beetle can fire its jet up to 20 times in succession.

Some **ladybug larvae** produce sticky silk threads that can tie up the mouths of ant attackers.

Carrion beetles live on decaying animal bodies, crawling with harmful bacteria. They protect themselves from the bacteria by releasing an ammonia mixture—rather like a really powerful cleaning fluid.

270°

How far a bombardier beetle can rotate its jet to aim at an enemy.

POOP DEFENSE

Some beetle larvae smear poop on their backs as a kind of stinky chemical defense.

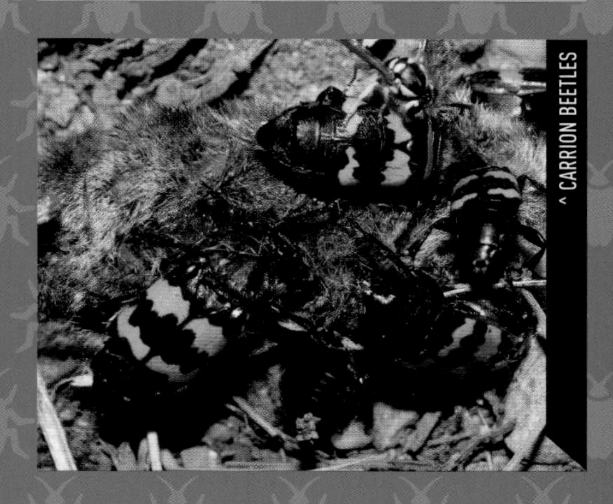

^ CARRION BEETLES

HOT *STUFF!*

The bombardier beetle isn't the only insect to shoot out chemicals, but it's the only one that can make its chemicals hot.

IT'S A RECORD!

FAST SHOOTER

The bombardier beetle can shoot out its jet a record five times faster than any other insect.

EJECTOR BEETLE

To escape an enemy, a **stenus bipunctatus** beetle dips its abdomen, then spurts out explosive chemicals to shoot itself backward.

INSECT SUPER-TRAVEL

Some insects have navigation superpowers. They journey for thousands of miles every year, finding their way to the same locations.

MONARCH BUTTERFLY

Every year, millions of monarch butterflies migrate from the Rocky Mountains region of the USA down to the Oyamel fir forest in Mexico, to spend the winter.

SCIENTISTS TRACK THE MIGRATION OF THE BUTTERFLIES BY TAGGING THEM WITH A TINY STICKER. EACH STICKER IS PRINTED WITH AN ID NUMBER.

THE MONARCHS USE THEIR ANTENNAE TO SENSE THE DIRECTION OF THE SUN, HELPING THEM GO SOUTHWARD. THEY CAN ALSO SENSE THE EARTH'S MAGNETIC FIELD.

ANYONE WHO SEES A MONARCH BUTTERFLY WITH AN ID NUMBER ON ITS HINDWING CAN REPORT THE LOCATION SIGHTING TO HELP TRACK THE PROGRESS OF THE MONARCHS

FACT FILE

MONARCH MIGRATION

1. The monarch butterflies start their journey in the fall. It is triggered by cooler temperatures and less daylight.

2. In spring, the butterflies migrate back to the southern USA, where the females lay their eggs.

3. The newly-hatched butterflies will eventually be the ones to continue the journey northward.

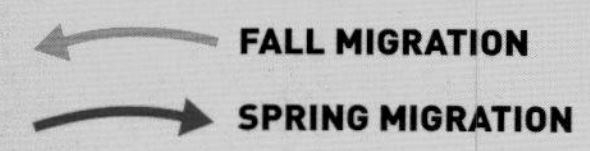

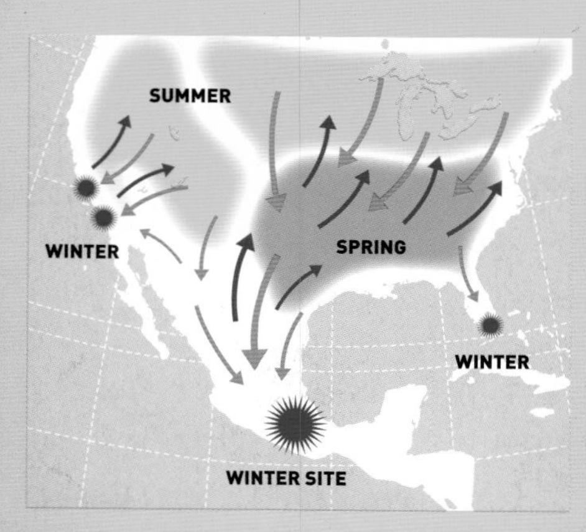

THE BUTTERFLIES GATHER ON THE FIR BRANCHES OF THE FOREST TREES TO OVERWINTER

SOULS IN FLIGHT

The arrival of the monarch butterflies in Mexico coincides with the Mexican Day of the Dead celebrations (below). Mexicans believe the monarchs represent the souls of past ancestors.

^ DAY OF THE DEAD CARNIVAL, MEXICO

UP TO
12 HOURS
A DAY

The time monarchs spend in the air on their journey.

SUPER *SENSE*

Fruit flies and monarch butterflies can sense the Earth's magnetic field using a special "magnetoreceptor" protein inside the eye. They use this supersense to help them navigate on long journeys.

Birds, bats, sea turtles, ants, bees, fruit flies, lobsters, newts, salmon, and sharks have the ability to sense the Earth's magnetic field. Some mammals, such as foxes and deer, may also be able to. Humans have the same magnetoreceptor eye protein, but don't appear to use it.

FRUIT FLY	FOX	HUMAN
= ✔	= ?	= ✘

200–400 MILES

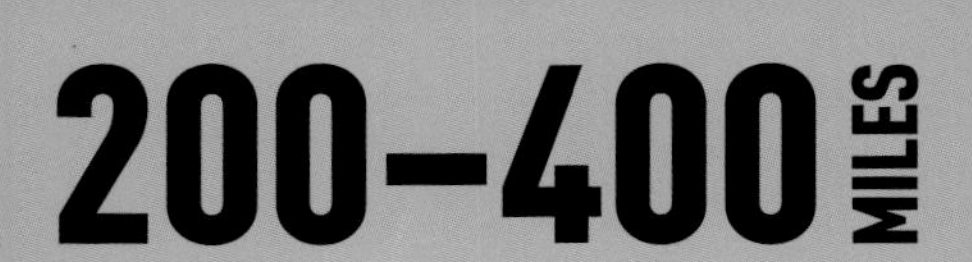

The distance that monarch butterflies can cover on a trip.

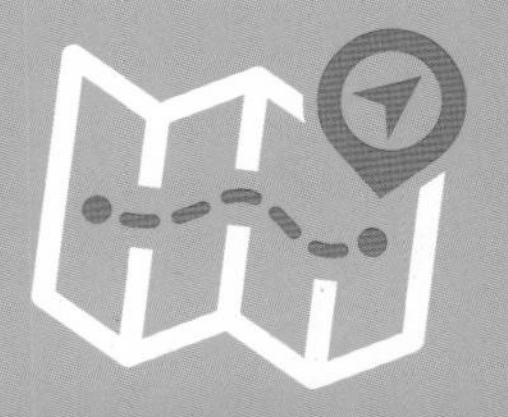

11,000 *FEET*

Glider pilots have reported seeing monarch butterflies flying at this height.

IT'S A **RECORD!**

11,000 MILES

The longest yearly journey-taker in the insect world is the globe skimmer dragonfly, which travels 11,000 miles back and forth between Africa and southern India.

THAT'S SO WEIRD!

Insects constantly surprise and amaze with their incredible skills. Many of them of look amazing, too. Downright weird and ugly, in fact!

Wetas are sometimes kept as pets. They are bred in zoos, too. Pet wetas like to chomp on carrots.

GIANT WETA

New Zealand's giant weta is the world's heaviest insect. Its Maori name—*wetapunga*—means "god of the ugly things."

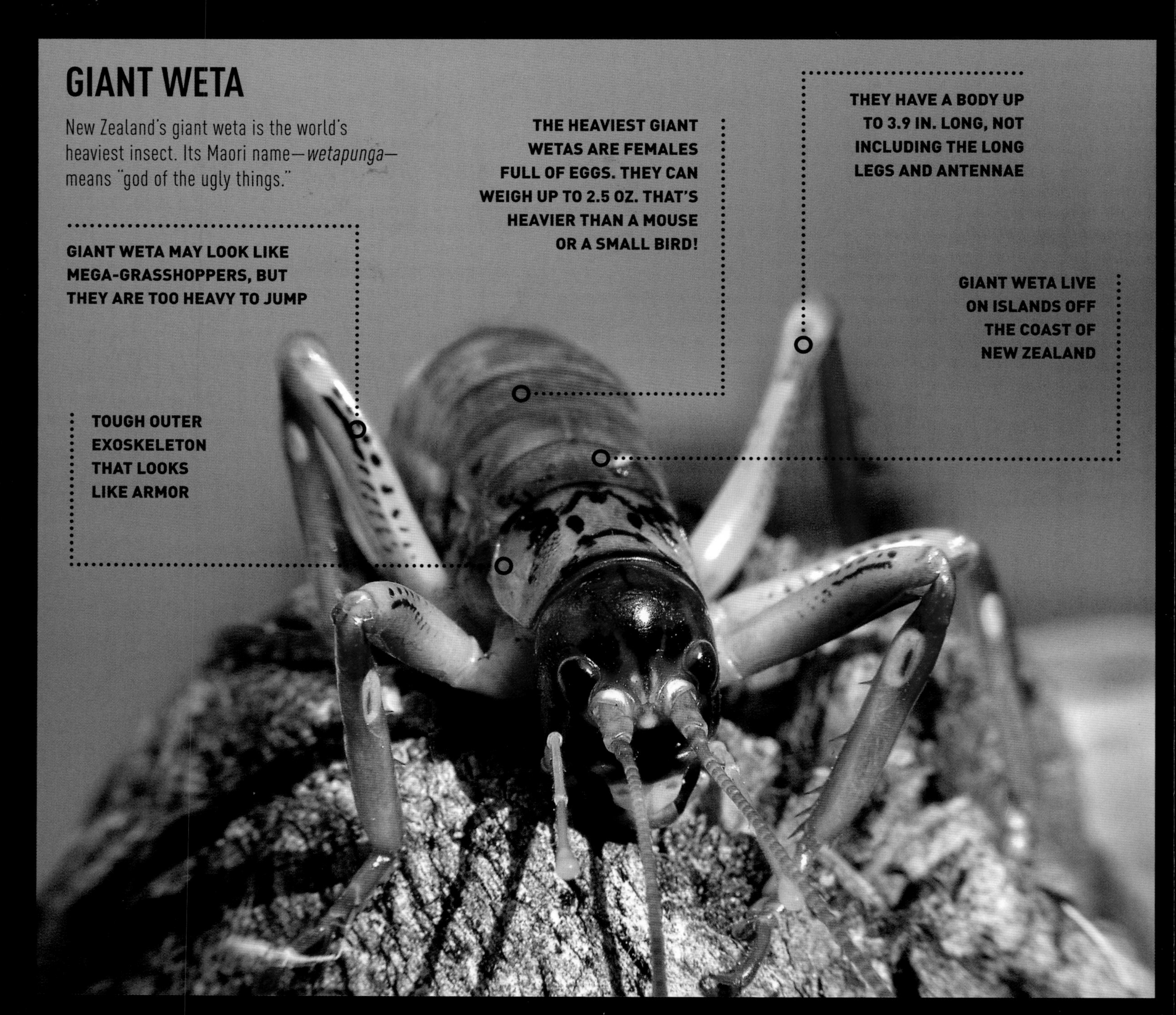

BIG MOUTH! *(LEFT)*
The **puss moth caterpillar's** head looks like a gaping mouth with two black eyes, to scare attackers. Its real head is poking out of the "mouth."

STAY AWAY! *(RIGHT)*
The **Cambodian lanternfly bug's** red horn probably makes it look bigger to its enemies.

BIGHEAD BUG *(BELOW)*
The **buffalo treehopper** gets its name because its head is wide like a buffalo's head. It is trying to mimic a thorn so that it doesn't get eaten as it sits on a branch eating tree sap.

SNAKE TIPS *(ABOVE)*
The **Atlas moth** has wing tips that look like a snake's head, ready to strike. It's sometimes nicknamed the cobra moth.

FLOWERY HUNTER *(LEFT)*
The **yellow ambush bug** has a complicated body that helps to disguise it as a flower.

GLOSSARY

ABDOMEN The end section of an insect's body, behind the thorax

AMBER Fossilized tree resin. Insects sometimes get trapped in resin, and their bodies become part of amber fossils.

ANTENNAE Insect body parts attached to the head, which are used for touch, taste, and smell

BROOD CELLS Cells found in a bees' nest, where eggs are laid and babies hatch

CARBON DIOXIDE A gas breathed out by mammals. Mosquitoes can detect it.

CERCI Pointed body parts at the end of an insect's body, used to sense danger from behind

CHRYSALIS A hard body-covering made by a caterpillar to hide and protect itself as it changes into a butterfly

COCOON A container of silk made by a caterpillar to hide itself as it changes into a butterfly

COLONY A group of insects living and working together

COMPOUND EYE An eye made up of many small lenses

DIGESTIVE SYSTEM The parts of the body that process food

DRONE A male bee

ELYTRA The hard wing cases of a beetle

ENZYME A chemical substance produced by an animal

EXOSKELETON The hard covering on the outside of an insect's body

FOREWINGS The front wings of a flying insect, such as a beetle

FRENULUM A section that connects the forewing and the hindwing of a moth

GLAND A body part that produces chemicals

HEMOLYMPH Fluid that circulates around an insect, like blood

HIBERNATE To spend the winter dormant (inactive)

HONEYCOMB A structure of six-sided cells, made by bees to store honey

HINDWINGS The back wings of a flying insect, such as a beetle

IMAGINAL DISC A group of cells inside a caterpillar's body that will eventually help it become a butterfly

LARVAE Baby insects that will completely change their shape when they grow into adults

LUCIFERIN A chemical produced by a firefly. It makes light but not heat.

MAGNETORECEPTOR An eye part that enables an animal to sense the Earth's magnetic field

MANDIBLES Insect jaws

METAMORPHOSIS When an insect larva (baby) changes shape completely to become an adult

MICRON A tiny unit of measurement. A human hair is 100 microns wide.

MIGRATION A yearly return journey made to a different location

MOLTING The process where an insect loses its old skin, hair, or feathers

NECTAR Sugary liquid produced by plants. Many insects drink nectar.

NIT An empty egg case left by a hatched head louse

NOCTURNAL A creature that is awake at night

NYMPH A baby insect that will only partly change shape as it grows into an adult

OCELLI Simple insect eyes that can detect light and shadow

OMMATIDIUM The name for the tiny lenses in the compound eye of an insect

OOTHECA An egg capsule produced by some insects, such as cockroaches

OVERWINTER To spend, or survive the winter months

PARASITE An animal or plant that lives off another animal or plant

PETIOLE The waist of a wasp

PHEROMONE A scented chemical produced by the body

POLLEN The substance produced by flowers and eaten by some insects

PROBOSCIS A tubelike tongue for sipping nectar

PROLEGS Stubby little leglike structures on a caterpillar's body

PRONOTUM A body section that protects the head of a ladybug

QUEEN The female egg-layer in an insect colony

SEGMENT A small section of something, such as the sections of an insect's leg

SPIRACLES Tiny holes on an insect's body, through which it breathes

STRIDULATION When an insect such as a cricket or a katydid rubs body parts together to make a noise

TERMITARIUM A termite nest

THORAX The middle section of an insect's body

TUBERCLES Nodules (fleshy knobs) on the body of an insect

TYMBALS Tiny drumlike organs on the abdomen of a cicada. It flexes them to make a clicking noise.

WORKER A female bee who doesn't lay eggs

INDEX

ACKNOWLEDGMENTS

PICTURE CREDITS:

KEY – tl top left, tc top center, tr top right, cl center left, c center, cr center right, bl bottom left, bc bottom center, br bottom right.,

© Shutterstock: 4b NH, 4tl Protasov AN, 4tr Tomatito, 4c piotreknik, 4br Sebastian Janicki, 6c Andrey Pavlov, 7tl Christian Vinces, 9tl Kletr, 8c ninii, 9bl Steven Ellingson, 10c seeyou, 11c Vitalii Hulai, 11b smuay, 12c Aleksandr Kurganov, 12cl ULKASTUDIO, 12b William Ritchie, 13bl Andrea Izzotti, 13tr Dancestrokes, 14c devil79sd, 15t ShaunWilkinson, 15tr Protasov AN, 15c Sebastian Kaulitzki, 15br Julia Kuznetsova, 17tr Elizabeth A.Cummings, 17bl matteo sani, 18c hagit berkovich, 19br twobee, 20c Laszlo Csoma, 20bl Pan Xunbin, 20br jaroslava V, 21tr Pan Xunbin, 21bc Noradoa, 23bl Alex James Bramwell, 23r Bruce MacQueen, 24c Brian Lasenby, 24tr Potapov Alexander, 25tl Eric Isselee, 25br Rostislav Kralik, 26c wonderisland, 27cr NH, 27cb Sergey Goruppa, 28c Jasper_Lensselink_Photography, 29tl Vladimir Zadvinskii, 29c IgorGolovniov, 30c Cosmin Manci, 31br Ermolaev Alexander, 33cl wonderisland, 33tr chakkrachai nicharat, 34br bearsky23, 35tr mrfiza, 37tl Sebastian Janicki, 37c Alexey V Smirnov, 38c V. J. Matthew, 38cr Henrik Larsson, 38bcl Breadmaker, 38br Howard Sandler, 39cr Henrik Larsson, 39bl David Papazian, 39bc Protasov AN, 39br Sebastian Kaulitzki, 40tr arka38, 41tc Protasov AN, 41c Albin Ebert, 42cl Tomatito, 42br irin-k, 43tr Marco Uliana, 45cr smuay, 45c Everett Historical, 45r N. F. Photography, 45br Ansis Klucis, 46b Melissa King, 47tl Eric Isselee, 47c Gucio_55, 47bl jigkofoto, 47br Andy Lidstone, 48bl JIANG HONGYAN, 49cr Sebastian Janicki, 49bc ChinKC, 50c alslutsky, 51tc piotreknik, 51br Madlen, 52bl Brandon Alms, 52c Cathy Keifer, 52b HTU, 53cl HTU, 54c Wasan Ritthawon, 55c Christian Musat, 56bl dalmingo , 56c Noradoa, 57bl pkproject, 57tr Milagli, 57c Kobby Dagan, 58c Graham R Prentice

© istock: 4bl vblinov, 7c StevenEllingson, 7br GlobalP, 8bl GlobalP, 9t Jan-Otto, 9tr belchonock, 9cb GlobalP, 9br Henrik_L, 11tr stevelenzphoto, 11tr Tetiana Ryshchenko, 15bl estt, 16c Antagain, 17tl BlackAperture, 17c dennisvdw, 19tr Mathisa_s, 19c User10095428_393, 22c CathyKeifer, 23tl defun, 23ct WebSubstance, 23c Henrik_L, 23br kunakos, 25cr GlobalP, 27tr BLUEXHAND, 31ct hooky13, 31c LindaMarieB, 32c wrobel27, 33c WebSubstance, 33br GlobalP, 34c Lightwriter1949, 35tl wxin, 35c sorsillo, 35cb paulrommer, 36c suwich, 37tr Bavorndej, 37br kavisimi, 38cl Anest, 38bl tfoxfoto, 38bcr KatarzynaBialasiewicz, 40bc ruvanboshoff, 41br kidsada Manchinda, 42tr ajball18, 43c Henrik_L, 43cb casadaphoto, 44c Henrik_L, 45ct mikeinlondon, 46cl Vitalii Hulai, 46c Vitalii Hulai, 46cr ErikKarits, 48tr Charly_Morlock, 49tc Steing, 49bl indigojt, 49br GlobalP, 51c towlake, 53tr ivkuzmin, 53c Atelopus, 53br OJ_Berlin, 55tr Vitalii Hulai, 55cr Wirepec, 56b Nicola Gordon, 59tl vblinov, 59c Rainbohm, 59tr number1411, 59bl StevenEllingson, 59br alle

© Wikimedia Commons: 38c Daiju Azuma

All other vector art © Shutterstock, © istock and Dynamo Limited